*In Him Is Life*

# Cross and Crown Series of Spirituality

GENERAL EDITOR

*Very Reverend John L. Callahan, O.P., S.T.M.*

LITERARY EDITOR

*Reverend Jordan Aumann, O.P., S.T.D.*

NUMBER 8

# IN HIM IS LIFE

BY *Ernest Mura*, F.S.V.

TRANSLATED BY

*Angeline Bouchard*

B. HERDER BOOK CO.

*15 & 17 South Broadway, St. Louis 2, Mo.*
AND *33 Queen Square, London, W. C.*

This is a translation of *L'humanité vivifiante du Christ*, by Ernest Mura, F.S.V., published by Emmanuel Vitte, Lyon and Paris. All rights reserved.

M93hE

IMPRIMI POTEST

Edward L. Hughes, O.P., S.T.M.
*Provincial*

NIHIL OBSTAT

J. S. Considine, O.P., S.T.M.
*Censor Deputatus*

IMPRIMATUR

✠ Samuel Cardinal Stritch
*Archbishop of Chicago*

April 20, 1956

Library of Congress Catalog Card Number: 56-10797

COPYRIGHT 1956 BY B. HERDER BOOK CO.

*Printed in the United States of America*
*by Vail-Ballou Press, Inc., Binghamton, New York*

# *Contents* ❧

|  |  | PAGE |
|---|---|---|
| INTRODUCTION | . . . . . . . . . . . | 1 |

CHAPTER
| 1 | FROM THE TRINITY TO THE WORD INCARNATE . . . | 7 |
| 2 | THE TESTIMONY OF SCRIPTURE . . . . . . . | 22 |
| 3 | IN THE LIGHT OF THEOLOGY . . . . . . . . | 32 |
| 4 | COMMUNION WITH THE MYSTERIES OF CHRIST . . . | 42 |
| 5 | THROUGH THE THEOLOGICAL VIRTUES . . . . . | 56 |
| 6 | THE WELLSPRINGS OF THE LITURGY . . . . . . | 73 |
| 7 | THE EUCHARISTIC SACRIFICE . . . . . . . . | 88 |
| 8 | THE BREAD OF LIFE . . . . . . . . . | 106 |
| 9 | QUICKENED BY THE BLOOD OF THE LAMB . . . . | 127 |
| 10 | TO CHRIST THROUGH MARY . . . . . . . . | 140 |
| 11 | THE ROSARY . . . . . . . . . . . | 160 |
| 12 | LIVING WITH CHRIST AND HIS MOTHER . . . . . | 177 |
| 13 | FRATERNAL CHARITY AND THE APOSTOLATE . . . | 197 |
| 14 | FRUITS OF LIFE . . . . . . . . . . | 215 |

# Introduction ✠

THE supernatural life of the soul is man's greatest treasure, for the life of grace makes us saints, children of God, and men who participate in God's own life. Where shall we seek this life? And once we have found it, how shall we nurture it to its plenitude?

The way we answer these questions will depend upon our notion of what the supernatural life is. Many souls base their interior life on the practice of the virtues, particularly the moral virtues, on generous efforts to correct their faults, and on the relentless combat against their evil tendencies. They seek perfection within themselves by making their will flexible and by learning to control their passions, so that in the end they may enjoy the interior peace that comes from complete self-mastery.

Ascesis—war against the passions and training of the will—is necessary, in fact indispensable, for the attainment of perfection. It would be a dangerous illusion to disregard this truth. Yet ascesis does not constitute holiness nor the life of the soul. God, in His loving providence, has chosen "to re-establish all things in Christ, both those in the heavens and those on the earth," [1] and hence our perfection and holiness are to be found not in man but "in

---
[1] Eph. 1:10.

1

Christ Jesus, who has become for us God-given wisdom, and justice, and sanctification, and redemption." [2] Christ is our life,[3] as St. Paul says over and over in many different ways. It is in Him that the Father has chosen us, "that we should be holy and without blemish in His sight." [4]

Hence, the center of our life and activity must not be within ourselves, but in Jesus, the Word made flesh, "full of grace and of truth." [5] Even if we developed our virtues to the point of heroism, we should have labored to no purpose if these efforts made us forget Him who alone must be our life, our virtue, and our holiness. We should have pursued an empty shadow of human perfection and lost sight of the divine Reality in whom alone lies all holiness. "I am the way, and the truth, and the life." [6]

Jesus, the Son of God made man, came into our midst to give us life, and to give it to us more abundantly.[7] He is the exemplar of the perfection toward which we must strive and the perfect image to which we were "predestined to become conformed." [8] In Him God has chosen us "before the foundation of the world, that we should be holy and without blemish in His sight." [9] But Christ is also the source of this divine life within us, for this life was in Him from the beginning.[10] Moreover, His sacred humanity, which is the instrument of His divinity, is the channel through which this river of life is poured into our souls.

It is clear, therefore, that the humanity of Christ is our great treasurer. Our perfection and holiness must consist in uniting ourselves to this sacred humanity, in communing

[2] I Cor. 1:30.
[3] Cf. Gal. 2:20; Col. 3:4.
[4] Eph. 1:4.
[5] John 1:14.
[6] *Ibid.*, 14:6.
[7] Cf. John 10:10.
[8] Rom. 8:29.
[9] Eph. 1:4.
[10] Cf. John 1:4.

with its life and mysteries, and in applying its sanctifying power to our souls. Each of the mysteries of Christ's life, everything that He ever did—even the humblest of His actions and His most secret thoughts and desires—has become a source of life and grace for us.

Our souls should be inspired with unlimited trust and courage by the awareness of the following truths: Jesus, who is so close to us by reason of His humanity, is our life and holiness; in all our needs we shall find in Him light and strength, a cure and a means of sustenance; our divine Savior has chosen to be the supplement for all our inadequacies, the mainstay of all our weaknesses, the fullness that fills up our indigence, and the satisfaction of all our hungers and aspirations.

We need to understand these consoling truths and to nourish our souls with them. Such is the purpose of this book. We intend to present this doctrine briefly and decisively. The solid foundation on which we shall build will be the Gospels and the Epistles of St. Paul. We shall also look to St. Thomas to give us his profound and illuminating theological explanation of the doctrine. Finally, spiritual writers—especially the masters of the seventeenth-century French school—will show us the multiple applications and the unlimited possibilities of life-giving union with the mysteries of Christ, which they understood and actualized so well.

The liturgy also holds a privileged place in realizing the doctrine of union with Christ, for the liturgical life is the Church so far as it reproduces and continues the mysteries of the life of Jesus. Thus, the Holy Sacrifice of the Mass will lay first claim to our attention, since it is the heart of the entire liturgy. The Precious Blood also deserves special emphasis in this study of Christ's life-giving humanity, for not only did it nourish the corporeal life of Jesus, but it became in an eminent way the source and principle of the spiritual life of His Mystical Body. Through these mysteries will be revealed to us in all their vastness "the unfathomable riches of Christ" [11] about which St. Paul preached so eloquently.

An indispensable chapter would be missing if we did not show the role which the Mother of our Savior plays in the communication of her divine Son's life to us. Is she not our Mother too, the Mother of our souls, and therefore a giver of life and a heavenly intermediary between ourselves and the sole Mediator, Christ? And after we have given the doctrinal basis of Mary's part in our life-giving union with Jesus, we shall devote a special chapter to the Holy Rosary as a practical expression of this Marian mediation. The riches of the supernatural life contained in the Rosary, through union with the mysteries of Jesus and Mary, should be well understood by devout souls.

In our concluding chapters we shall strive to place the entire life of the Christian, in all its aspects, within the framework and under the sanctifying influence of the life of Christ. If we follow life's paths with Jesus and Mary we shall learn that there is nothing profane in an authentically Christian life, nothing that may be excluded from the grace of our Savior, who came among us so that we might live by Him. We shall find that fraternal charity and the exercise of an intense apostolate, to which the Church is at the present time urging all her children, are the best means of submitting our daily life to the action of our divine Head.

Finally, to stress the essentially practical application of the doctrine we have presented, we shall deduce a few

[11] Eph. 3:8.

conclusions which we believe will be helpful to all who consider them seriously. These conclusions will show how every word spoken by Jesus, as well as every particle of revealed doctrine is "spirit and life." [12]

May the Most Blessed Virgin, whom Pope Pius XII has called the "most holy Mother of all Christ's members," [13] make clear to all Christian souls the economy of this hidden mystery of our vital and sanctifying bond with Christ and with His sacred humanity and powerfully inspire them to unite themselves to this living Sacrament of all grace and holiness, so that they may be consummated in God according to the Apostle's words: "in order that you may be filled unto all the fullness of God." [14]

[12] John 6:64.
[13] *Mystici Corporis,* Par. 129 (English translation published by the Paulist Press, 401 West 59th St., New York).
[14] Eph. 3:19.

# CHAPTER 1 ✍

# *From the Trinity to the Word Incarnate*

"NOW this is everlasting life, that they may know Thee, the one true God, and Him whom Thou hast sent, Jesus Christ." [1] To know God, to bask in His light, to allow ourselves to be vivified by His Word, who became man to reveal His Father to us—this is the life to which we aspire. This is the divine and eternal life for which we were created and to which we are called by God. To know God with a loving knowledge, by faith and obscure contemplation even in this life and in the face-to-face encounter of the beatific vision in heaven, what a sublime vocation for the children of men!

This life of knowledge and love has its source in God Himself, in the Blessed Trinity, for God is eternal, subsisting life. But the fountainhead of this life among us is Jesus Christ, the Son of God made man. The Word receives the life of the Father in its fullness and then causes His sacred humanity to participate in this divine life by means of the hypostatic union, in order to transmit the divine life to us as through a living instrument.

Before speaking of our divine life through Christ, we

[1] John 17:3.

7

shall first contemplate this life in God Himself: in the
unity of the three divine Persons and in the Incarnate
Word living among us.

St. Thomas tells us that God is His own life, just as He is
His own being and His own eternally operative intellect
and will. But what do we mean when we say "to live"?
Philosophers give us an answer which is in accord with
common sense. To live, they say, is to move oneself, to
possess within oneself the principle of one's operations,[2]
in contrast to the passivity of inert beings that receive all
their movement and activity from without. A stone will roll
wherever it is kicked; iron responds mechanically to the
pull of the magnet; the interplay of physical forces in nature—from cosmic evolutions to chemical changes—consists in these lifeless actions and reactions. For all its
marvelous activity, inert matter cannot begin to measure
up to the perfection of life, even in its lowest forms.

Plants, animals, and especially men have been endowed
with a nobler activity by their divine Creator. They move
and act by themselves. Growth, reproduction, sight, feeling,
desire, will, and love constitute perfections of action which
surpass anything attainable in the world of inert matter,
for all its vast resources.

In man, whose soul is spiritual, and even more in the
angels, who are pure spirits, this immanence of operation,
this self-movement, reaches a degree of perfection which
in a certain respect touches the infinite. Since the intellect
is not confined within the narrow boundaries of matter, it
can receive into itself, by a kind of luminous transparence,
the perfection of all beings; it can spiritually take on their
diverse forms and communicate with the entire universe.
Then the will, stimulated by the activity of the intellect,

[2] Cf. *Summa theol.*, Ia, q. 18, a. 3.

is united through love with all that is beautiful, noble, great, and good. The good of all things becomes the will's good and its food, so to speak.

God's life is infinite in the strictest sense of the word. His supreme intellect and His perfect, limitless will are identical with His infinite being. God not only has life, He *is* life. He is life in a measureless degree that exceeds the grasp of our puny created minds. The life of God is an eternal and immutable vision of His subsisting beauty; it is the infinite and supremely beatifying love of His boundless goodness. It is a perfect life which had no beginning and will have no end, a life without change or succession, a life of ineffable contemplation and love.

"I live, saith the Lord." [3] This is the solemn attestation of His most perfect life, as He so often gives it in Scripture. "For He is the living and eternal God forever," says Daniel.[4] And through Him alone every be-souled creature lives and breathes: "I will kill and I will make to live." [5]

But the divine life has a still more marvelous aspect which human reason could never have surmised if divine goodness had not seen fit to reveal it to us. God possesses His life in the society of the three divine Persons. The Father eternally communicates this life to the Son whom He begets, and through the Son to the Holy Ghost who proceeds from the Father and the Son.

God's life is knowledge and love. In knowing Himself, the Father expresses Himself by a perfect intellectual image. This image is His Word, the pure reflection of His supreme perfection, and "the brightness of His glory." [6] The life of the Father overflows by way of knowledge, and this overflowing is a real generation whose term is "the

---

[3] Isa. 49:18; Ezech. 5:11.     [4] Dan. 6:26; 14:24.
[5] Deuter. 32:39.     [6] Heb. 1:3.

only-begotten Son, who is in the bosom of the Father." [7]

The Father and the Son are distinct from one another by reason of their opposite relations of active and passive generation,[8] but at the same time they are united by a common love. In their mutual love, in their ineffable transport toward the infinite good of their common essence, the Father and Son breathe forth, so to speak, a breath of unutterable love. This breath or *spiritus* is the Holy Spirit, the subsistent love of the Father and the Son, and the consummation of the Trinitarian life of the eternal One.

Some Protestants have held that a knowledge of the mystery of the Blessed Trinity is of no practical importance for the supernatural life. They have declared that God revealed this supreme mystery to us only to humble our reason by forcing it to acknowledge its helplessness, or at most to serve as a guide for the understanding of the other mysteries such as the Incarnation and the mission of the Holy Ghost.

This is a grave error. Belief in the mystery of the three divine Persons is the wellspring of the whole supernatural life. Is not the supernatural life a participation in the intimate life of the most adorable Trinity? It is by the power of the Trinity that the soul is regenerated at baptism. The newly baptized Christian is consecrated to the Blessed Trinity and becomes the temple of the Blessed Trinity.

From the moment of baptism, the divine life of the Christian is progressively orientated toward the one and triune God who created us, redeemed us, and sanctifies us —toward the Father whose children we are, toward the

---

[7] John 1:18.

[8] The Father is He who speaks His Word, He who begets; the Son is He who is spoken as the Word, the Begotten.

Son, our divine Savior and Master, and toward the Holy Ghost, the architect of all holiness.

It is unfortunately true that many Christians fail to reach their goal, preferring to remain in the path of mediocrity, and that many fall after having made great progress. But in the mystical ascent of those who wholeheartedly embrace their Christian vocation, the fullness of the supernatural life can best be described as the flowing into their souls of the intimate life of the Blessed Trinity. The contemplation of this mystery lights up the summit of our spiritual life here on earth and is consummated in the mystical marriage which is the prelude to the face-to-face contemplation of the Blessed Trinity in heaven.

But let us not anticipate. We must remember that God's life, before it began to flow into our redeemed souls, was communicated in its fullness to the human nature of the Word. "In Him was life." [9] In the Word is the totality of life. "And the Word was made flesh, and dwelt among us. . . . full of grace and truth." [10] This grace is the divine life possessed by the sacred humanity of Jesus in a measure that is infinite in a certain respect. It is from Jesus that we receive our participation in the divine life, as Dom Marmion says: "The same divine life which proceeds from the Father into the Son and from the Son into the humanity of Jesus, will circulate, through Christ, in all who will accept it; it will draw them even into the bosom of the Father, where Christ has gone before us." [11]

"Let us therefore draw near with confidence to the throne of grace," [12] as St. Paul calls the Son of God made

[9] John 1:4.  [10] *Ibid.*, 1:14.
[11] *Christ the Life of the Soul*, pp. 6–7 (St. Louis: B. Herder Book Co., 1925).
[12] Heb. 4:16.

man. But we must first learn to know the Word Incarnate, the mystery of His hypostatic union, His infinite holiness, and the riches of life that He possesses in His sacred humanity. Then we can communicate these mysteries to those who are called by the Father "to be adopted through Jesus Christ as His sons." [13] For "as many as received Him [Jesus Christ] He gave the power of becoming sons of God." [14]

To know Christ, the Son of God made man, is the foundation of the whole supernatural life. The Apostle reminded those who might be tempted to build their spiritual edifice on some other groundwork: "As a wise builder, I laid the foundation. . . . For other foundation no one can lay, but that which has been laid, which is Christ Jesus." [15]

Christ is first and above all the Son of God. Faith in His divinity is the starting point of the whole Christian life. It was our Savior Himself who demanded this explicit profession of faith from His Apostles: "Thou art the Christ, the Son of the living God." [16] He then showed His approval of this testimony by blessing St. Peter, who had given it: "Blessed art thou, Simon Bar-Jona, for flesh and blood has not revealed this to thee, but My Father in heaven." [17]

No one can describe the light and strength and joy that flood the soul of a Christian who can confidently say to his Savior, to the One who is his life: "Thou art the Son of the living God!" or more explicitly, with Dom Marmion: "O Jesus Christ, Incarnate Word, I cast myself down before Thee, because Thou art the Son of God, equal to the

[13] Eph. 1:5; cf. also Rom. 8:29.     [14] John 1:12.
[15] I Cor. 3:10–11.                    [16] Matt. 16:16.
[17] *Ibid.*, 16:17.

Father. Thou art indeed the Son of God, *Deum de Deo, lumen de lumine, Deum verum de Deo vero.* Thou art the beloved Son of the Father, in whom He is well pleased. I love and adore Thee!" [18] Faith in the divinity of Christ gives us strength to face the world and all the hostile powers of evil, for "this is the victory that overcomes the world, our faith." [19]

But Christ, the Son of God, is also the Son of man. The Word, who is equal to the Father, has become one of us in all things.[20] He was born of the Virgin Mary so that within her most pure womb He might become our brother in humanity. He possesses a body like ours, which was once subject to fatigue and suffering. In the first centuries of the Christian era certain heretics were scandalized by this. They preferred to hold that Christ's body was not real but only apparent. But if Christ were not really a man, then our redemption and the whole economy of man's salvation would be a mirage. On the contrary, we firmly declare, in the words of the Nicene Creed, that the Son of God came down from heaven for us men and for our salvation. The Gnostic heresy brings out in its own way something of the voluntary humiliation and infinite condescension implicit in the incarnation of the Word.

Jesus assumed a mortal body for the sole purpose of experiencing all our woes, except sin. As St. Paul says, He was "tried as we are in all things except sin." [21] For many long years He submitted to the fatigue of manual labor. People used to ask: "Is not this the carpenter's son?" [22] And again: "Is not this the carpenter, the son of Mary?" [23] By His own labor He redeemed and ennobled the painful

[18] *Op. cit.,* pp. 17–18.
[19] I John 5:4.
[20] Cf. Heb. 2:17.
[21] Heb. 4:15.
[22] Matt. 13:55.
[23] Mark 6:3.

toil of countless laborers in revolt against their fate and
He laid the foundation of the Christian social restoration
that is still in the process of fulfillment.

Jesus suffered hunger in the desert and He experienced
thirst. He asked the Samaritan woman to give Him a few
drops of water, and on the cross He proclaimed His thirst
in tones of anguish. Christ our Brother fell from weariness
by the roadside. During His apostolic travels He stopped,
just as we do, to recover His breath. On the road to Golgotha He fell to the ground. The heaviness of sleep overcame Him and He slept in the boat while the tempest
terrified His disciples.

Above all, Jesus suffered in His body all the tortures
that a delicate human organism can endure: His head was
pierced with thorns when He was crowned with a diadem of
mockery; He felt the lash and the rod during His scourging, and later the terrible impact of the nails in His divine
limbs. Yes, Christ, our eldest Brother, was endowed with
real flesh by the mystery of the Incarnation. "The Word
was made flesh!" [24]

Into this body the Son of God received a human soul, a
spiritual, immortal soul like our own, which was the principle of His human and natural life; a soul that He was to
yield up to His Father as the supreme proof of His filial
love when He cried out from the cross: "Father, into Thy
hands I commend My spirit." [25] For we must not forget that
He had the power to lay down His life and to take it up
again.[26]

Christ's soul was endowed with all the operative powers
that enrich our own: a penetrating mind, a free will, interior and exterior sense faculties, affective and appetitive

[24] John 1:14.                          [25] Luke 23:46.
[26] Cf. John 10:18.

powers. From the first instant of His Incarnation, all of His powers were vitally actuated. His mind was more luminous than that of the most outstanding genius; His will was inflexible in its movement toward the good and in its absolute revulsion against evil. His heart was tender and generous, capable of the deepest sufferings, as the Agony in the Garden has proved to us.

The human heart of Jesus was the focal point of all His sentiments as man. Goodness, fidelity, and virtue made Him happy. He thrilled with delight at the noble faith of the Canaanite woman and He found happiness in the friendship of St. John. There was Lazarus, too, whose death He honored with His tears. Jesus experienced emotions of sadness and anguish. His heart was deeply wounded by the atrocity of Judas' kiss. He trembled with fear in anticipation of His passion and, as St. Paul tells us, He mingled tears with His blood.[27]

Jesus has thus revealed Himself to be a perfect man as well as a perfect God. As the Son of God begotten of the Father, He is the model and principle of the adoptive sonship to which we are called by participation in His natural sonship. As the Son of man through Mary, He is the Mediator who is very close to us and who saves us and leads us to the Father.

But there is more to be said concerning the Word Incarnate. Nestorius admitted that there was both a divine and a human reality in Christ, but he distinguished the divine from the human to the point of separating them into two persons, united merely by a moral bond. Accordingly, the person of Christ was a complete and independent being, and in Him by a presence of love and grace, dwelt the uncreated Person of the Son of God. There is a radical

[27] Cf. Heb. 5:7.

error in this view. It amounts to a denial of the mystery of
the Incarnation and it destroys the entire economy of the
Redemption. For Jesus has saved us only because the work
of His humanity is the work of God Himself in the unity
of a single Person.

The answer to the Nestorian heresy is to be found in the
words of St. John: "And the Word was made flesh." He
who subsists as the Word in the bosom of the Father, He
who is the Son of God, has assumed our flesh and our human nature. And this sacred humanity, since it has no
being or personality of its own, exists and subsists through
the Word, is assumed by the Word, and is in some way
drawn into the being and the personality of the Word,
who communicates to it His own subsistence. This doctrine
is fundamental to the Christian life.

Because the same Christ is God and man and because the
Person of the Word has assumed our flesh and our human
nature, the actions and sufferings of this nature are the
actions and sufferings of God. When Jesus did manual
labor, this work certainly proceeded from His humanity,
but since His humanity exists only in the Word and
through the being of the Word, it was the labor of God,
and therefore a work of infinite worth. When Jesus prayed,
His prayer proceeded actively from His holy soul, but
strictly speaking it was God's prayer, the prayer of the Son
Himself, who is always "heard because of His reverent submission." [28]

This is the crux of the great mystery. It is the source of
life and of all good things for our sinful humanity. We
shall see more precisely how this is so in the following
chapters.

The hypostatic union must govern our whole attitude

[28] Heb. 5:7.

toward the God-man. In the presence of Jesus we fall on our knees in profound adoration, like the man born blind. Everything about Christ is worthy of adoration, inasmuch as it belongs to the Son of God. It is clear that the divinity of the Word is adorable and deserves the supreme cult of latria.[29] Equally adorable is His sacred humanity. His most holy soul, His most pure body, His divine heart, His wounds and His blood—all are worthy of adoration, as are all the acts of His humanity: those of the Child who whimpered in the manger or smiled in His Mother's arms, those of the divine Adolescent who labored by Joseph's side, and those of the Man of Sorrows who expired on the cross. The liturgical cult of the Church as well as the personal devotion of interior souls find in these things a substantial and inexhaustible food.

From its personal union with the Word, the human nature of Christ receives a supernatural enrichment, a galaxy of gifts. Such is the dowry which the Son of God brings to His humanity: riches of grace and lofty knowledge which reflect the light of divinity.

Theology distinguishes a threefold grace in Jesus as man and a threefold knowledge in His human intellect. His divine nature, on the other hand, possesses the infinite knowledge and holiness that are common to the three Persons. In the first place, there is in Jesus' human nature the substantial holiness that is called the grace of union. It is identified with the hypostatic union, which we have just been discussing. The grace of union is the unction of divinity of which Scripture speaks.[30] Jesus Himself pointed it out in the synagogue of Nazareth when He read the passage from Isaias: "The Spirit of the Lord is upon Me

[29] Latria is the cult of adoration reserved for God alone.
[30] Cf. Ps. 44:8.

because He has anointed Me, to bring good news to the poor." [31] It is an unction that consecrated the humanity of Christ in its innermost fibers, conferring upon it an infinite dignity and holiness. It was at once a priestly and a royal unction that constituted Jesus the eternal Priest and the King of all creation. Through the hypostatic union, Jesus became the Mediator between God and man, that is, the necessary Pontiff of all creation before God. And through the infinite elevation of His human nature, Christ became the Man par excellence, the King and Head of all creatures, in the words of the Apostle, "the firstborn of every creature." [32]

The grace of union is situated on the level of being itself, but as a consequence of this grace, another grace sanctifies Jesus' powers of operation and causes a very lofty supernatural life to permeate His soul and His faculties. This is sanctifying grace, together with the gifts and the virtues which infallibly accompany it. St. Thomas describes Christ's sanctifying grace as being infinite, so to speak. [33] Jesus needed this sanctifying grace so that His human nature might have, in addition to its subsistence in the Word, a created participation in the divine nature and a resemblance to God that would make it capable of God-like operations just as ours has. All the infused virtues [34] and all the gifts of the Holy Ghost are joined to it, thus making Jesus the consummate model of all holiness. That is why He said to His disciples: "Learn from Me." [35] This perfection of His human powers and their freedom from all weakness under the influence of His plenitude of grace

---

[31] Luke 4:18; cf. Isa. 61:1.       [32] Col. 1:15.

[33] Cf. *Summa theol.*, IIIa, q. 17, a. 11.

[34] With the exception of faith and hope, which are incompatible with the vision of God.

[35] Matt. 11:29.

made it possible for Him to throw down a divine challenge to His enemies: "Which of you can convict Me of sin?" [36]

The superabundant grace of Christ was to be poured out upon all His "brothers" in the human race in accordance with the wisdom of God, thus becoming His capital grace or the grace of Headship. The supernatural life of Jesus is poured out on all the members of His Mystical Body, quickening them with the Spirit of holiness and with the aspiration toward God which motivates all His actions as God-man.

St. John sums up the perfection of the Word made flesh when he says that we saw Him "full of grace and of truth." [37] In addition to His fullness of grace, He also possesses incomparable knowledge and wisdom. So great were His wisdom and knowledge that His astonished hearers cried out: "Never has man spoken as this man!" [38] Even today the greatest geniuses stand in admiration before His intellect, whose breadth and depth cannot be measured by any man. Even during His mortal life, Jesus' knowledge was perfected by the beatific vision and by God's own infinite knowledge.

We must distinguish three kinds of knowledge in the created intellect of Christ. His acquired knowledge is the lowest of the three, comparatively speaking, but even that is eminent. Jesus obtained this knowledge, just as we do, from the things about Him and by the efforts of His penetrating intellect. This experimental and abstractive knowledge brings the God-man very close to us and to the world in which we live. During His earthly life He proved He could acquire knowledge by expressing surprise at learning things He had not known before.

[36] John 8:46.  [37] *Ibid.*, 1:14.
[38] *Ibid.*, 7:46.

However, His redemptive mission demanded that He should have perfect knowledge of all that concerned His role as Savior and that He should have it from the start and not await the slow acquisition of facts and ideas. This infused knowledge came to Him from a twofold source. On the one hand He possessed knowledge through species or concepts received from God, as the angels and separated souls do. It belongs properly to Christ to have such knowledge because He is the Head of angels and men and because He was in the state of ultimate perfection from the first moment of His human life. Moreover, the beatific vision or immediate knowledge of the divine essence was strictly due to the Son of God as man and was the necessary prerogative of Him who came among us to be our way toward the goal and our guide to our homeland. "He who follows Me does not walk in the darkness, but will have the light of life." [39]

As a natural extension of this knowledge and holiness, Jesus possesses unlimited power over all material and spiritual beings, over men and societies. It is a power of command and of efficacious action. The sea and the winds obey Him, as do the angels and devils, either voluntarily or as the coerced executors of His sovereign commands. Did He not say when He was about to ascend to heaven: "All power in heaven and on earth has been given to Me"? [40]

And yet Jesus exercises His power chiefly upon our souls, by an action that is at once gentle and powerful, by a mysterious influence whose secret effects make themselves felt by the gradual growth and transformation of our souls. It is like the efficacious but hidden influence of the sun on the growth of plants. The Word made flesh, by an action

[39] John 8:12.                    [40] Matt. 28:18.

that knows no respite, communicates His divine life to us, makes us grow in grace and virtue, unites us ever more closely to Himself, and transforms us to His own likeness. He does all this, of course, in proportion to our docility— which is too often defective. He quickens us with His divine Spirit so that we shall some day be able to say with St. Paul: "It is now no longer I that live, but Christ lives in me." [41] It is a work of life and sanctification, whose fitting instrument is the sacred humanity of Jesus, united to the Word and acting through the Word. Let us now meditate more profoundly upon this truth.[42]

[41] Gal. 2:20.

[42] In this preliminary chapter we have done no more than give a substantial summary of the theology of the Word Incarnate, in order to provide us with a basis for the doctrine that we are about to set forth. For a more thorough understanding of this theology of the Word Incarnate, the reader is referred to works that deal with this subject *ex professo*. Cf. R. Garrigou-Lagrange, O.P., *Our Savior and His Love for Us* (St. Louis: B. Herder Book Company, 1951), especially chapters 11 and 12.

# CHAPTER 2 ✍

# *The Testimony of Scripture*

"NO one comes to the Father but through Me." [1] The whole movement of our supernatural life consists in going to the Father. "Our Father who art in heaven" is the first aspiration that the Holy Ghost, the author of all prayer,[2] inspires in every Christian heart. St. Paul tells us, "God has sent the Spirit of His Son into our hearts, crying 'Abba, Father.' " [3]

Our baptismal grace is the grace of the adoption of sons, which engrafts us upon Christ so that we may be the children of His Father's love. By making us members of the Mystical Body of Christ, the sacrament of regeneration makes us younger brothers of Jesus and adopted sons of His Father. That is why growth in grace consists in continually increasing our filial attitude toward our Father in heaven. As Jesus told His disciples: "Unless you turn and become like little children, you will not enter into the kingdom of heaven." [4] Humility and spiritual childhood are required of each and every Christian, for the very reason that we have but one Father in heaven.[5]

The Father is the term of our spiritual life as well as its

[1] John 14:6.  
[2] Cf. Rom. 8:26.  
[3] Gal. 4:6.  
[4] Matt. 18:3.  
[5] Cf. *Ibid.*, 23:9.

principle, for St. James tells us that "He has begotten us by the word of truth, that we might be, as it were, the first-fruits of His creatures."[6] It is to the Father that Jesus teaches us to pray in secret,[7] far from the eyes of men. It is the Father who is the sublime exemplar whom our Savior teaches us to imitate in the efficacious love we must have for both the good and the wicked: "You therefore are to be perfect, even as your heavenly Father is perfect."[8] He is the Father who dispenses His sunshine and His rain to the just and the wicked. If we do as He does, Jesus tells us that we shall be children of our Father in heaven.[9]

St. Paul echoes these words of the Master when he writes to the Ephesians on the subject of charity: "Be you, therefore, imitators of God, as very dear children."[10] And again to the Romans: "The Spirit Himself gives testimony to our spirit that we are sons of God."[11]

Thus, God is our Father. His gratuitous charity has led Him to bend down over our lowliness and unworthiness to adopt us as His children. Our devotion must therefore be a filial and obedient love for the Father in heaven.

But how shall we rise to such heights? How can we even aspire to it? To go to the Father, will we not need a heavenly ladder or at least an easy path? Jesus is both the ladder and the path. He is the way, as He Himself has told us.[12] He is the mystical ladder of Jacob by which the angels of God and the souls of Christians go and come until they reach the Father, as He explained to Nathaniel.[13]

In actual fact, if we would become children of the Father we must become brothers of His only Beloved, Jesus. The

---

[6] Jas. 1:18.
[7] Cf. Matt. 6:6.
[8] *Ibid.*, 5:48.
[9] Cf. *ibid.*, 5:45.
[10] Eph. 5:1.
[11] Rom. 8:16.
[12] Cf. John 14:6.
[13] Cf. *ibid.*, 1:51.

Father has only one Son, in whom He is well pleased.[14]
Therefore, in order to deserve the name of children of God
and to become worthy of bringing ineffable delight to the
Father, we must in some way immerse and lose ourselves
in the Sonship of Jesus. St. Thomas tells us: "No one can
be an adopted child unless he unites himself and cleaves
to the natural Son of God." [15]

This is also the teaching of Paul, who writes to the Ephesians: "Blessed be the God and Father of our Lord Jesus
Christ, who . . . presdestined us to be adopted through
Jesus Christ as His sons." [16] With even greater precision he
writes to the Galatians: "For you are all the children of
God through faith in Christ Jesus. For [note the causality
implied] all you who have been baptized into Christ, have
put on Christ." [17] How can we become the children of God
unless we put on, in holy baptism, the only Son, Christ
Jesus? Therein lies the fulfillment of our divine vocation of
which the Apostle speaks: "to become conformed to the
image of His Son." [18] The grace of our Christianity makes
us faithful replicas of the beloved Son, who is the perfect
image of His Father, the Word in which the Father expresses all His perfection, "the brightness of His glory," [19]
and the substantial imprint of His infinite Being. This
explains and justifies the sublime audacity of the saints,
such as St. Francis of Assisi and of a St. Therese of Lisieux.

We find the same teaching in St. John. He repeats with
insistence that we are children of God, but on one condition: that we receive the Only Son with love and faith,
that we receive the Word made flesh whom His own did
not receive. "To as many as received Him He gave the

[14] Cf. Matt. 3:17; 17:5.          [15] In Eph. 3:26.
[16] Eph. 1:3–5.                     [17] Gal. 3:26–27.
[18] Rom. 8:29.                      [19] Heb. 1:3.

power of becoming sons of God." [20] The necessary condition for sharing in the divine Sonship of Jesus is to receive and to welcome Him. But to do this, we must have faith, a living faith through which we welcome the Gift of God and live by Him.

In his first Epistle, St. John lays great stress on this gift of divine life through the Son. "God," he says, "has given us eternal life; and this life is in His Son. He who has the Son has the life. He who has not the Son has not the life." [21]

Our supernatural life is so completely contained in Jesus that to live this life we must possess Jesus Himself and live with Him in the bosom of the Father. How far this brings us from any egocentric concept of the spiritual life, which is completely orientated to the development of natural virtue and our own personality! The truth is that when we receive the Word of life and light through the grace of baptism, we are "born not of blood, nor of the will of the flesh, nor of the will of man, but of God." [22]

This vital union with the Son of God is what wins for us the love of our heavenly Father, the same love that He has for His Only-Begotten. Jesus assured His apostles of this in the sublime prayer which came forth from His priestly soul on the eve of His death: "That all may be one, even as Thou, Father, in Me and I in Thee; that they also may be one in us, that the world may believe that Thou hast sent Me. . . . That they may be perfected in unity, and that the world may know that Thou hast sent Me, and that Thou hast loved them even as Thou hast loved Me." [23] Jesus abiding in us, and the Father abiding in Jesus, His only Son: such is the astounding union that God has willed

[20] John 1:12.
[22] John 1:13.
[21] I John 5:11–12.
[23] *Ibid.*, 17:21–23.

between Himself and us. And the root of this sublime gift is love—the love of the Father for His beloved Son which He extends to us to implant in us the likeness of His Only-Begotten and to make us live by His life. This truth inspired Dom Marmion to write: "Never forget that Jesus Christ is everything and we are agreeable to the Father only in proportion as we are united to Him. . . . He is the golden bond of union between all creation and the adorable Trinity. As our dear St. Gertrude says, He is the harp through whose strings all praise must resound in order to be an agreeable harmony to the adorable Trinity." [24]

Elizabeth of the Trinity, inspired by her own particular grace, understood and practiced this doctrine of life in the footsteps of the great Apostle. To quote her own words: "It is no longer I that live, but He lives in me. I no longer want to live by my own life, but I want to be transformed into Jesus Christ so that when the Father bends down over me He will see the image of His beloved Son in whom He is well pleased." [25]

We can now understand the words of Jesus cited at the beginning of this chapter, which point out the direction of our whole supernatural life: "No one comes to the Father but through Me." But before the Son of God could become our way to the Father, our Mediator, and our oldest Brother who would lead us to the Father, He had to abase Himself to our level. He had to become one of us, a son of our sinful race. He had to assume our mortal flesh and dwell among us and through the channel of His humanity bring to us the riches of life and holiness whose

[24] Quoted in Dom Raymond Thibaut's biography, *Abbot Columba Marmion, A Master of the Spiritual Life* (St. Louis: B. Herder, 1949), pp. 91–92.

[25] Sister Elizabeth of the Trinity, *Reminiscences* (Newman, 1952).

source is in God. This is the reason for the Incarnation.

As St. John tells us, "The life eternal which was with the Father . . . has appeared to us." [26] It became visible and palpable [27] through the mystery of the Word made flesh, and it has been communicated to us so that "our fellowship may be with the Father, and with His Son Jesus Christ." [28] The beloved disciple appealed to his personal experience to inspire the hearts of the faithful to joyous exultation over these treasures of life that had been won for them. "What was from the beginning, what we have heard, what we have seen with our eyes, what we have looked upon and our hands have handled, of the Word of life, . . . we announce to you, in order that you also may have fellowship with us" [29] and participate in the life of the Father through the Son, "that you may rejoice, and our joy may be full." [30]

We have great cause for joy in this certitude of possessing the life of God Himself through Jesus, the Word Incarnate. For joy, as the Angelic Doctor teaches, proceeds from union with the good that we love,[31] and through grace we are united to the infinite Good and we possess the life of God.

"In [God] was life," [32] St. John writes, the eternal life of the adorable Trinity, a life of knowledge in God's ineffable contemplation of His infinite perfection which terminates in the generation of the Word, a life of beatifying love which springs up in a flame of charity from the Father and the Son, and from which the Holy Ghost proceeds. This life of knowledge and love, as we have seen, was com-

[26] I John 1:1–2.  
[27] Cf. *ibid.*, 1:3.  
[28] *Ibid.*  
[29] *Ibid.*, 1:1–3.  
[30] *Ibid.*, 1:4.  
[31] Cf. *Summa theol.*, IIa IIae, q. 28, a. 1.  
[32] John 1:4.

municated by the Word to His sacred humanity in a measure incomprehensible to man. For "the Word was made
flesh, and dwelt among us, . . . full of grace and of
truth." [33]

But this fullness of knowledge and holiness, this super-
abundance of divine life which flowed from the divinity of
the Word into His human nature, was destined, in the
order of divine wisdom, to be poured out upon us. We are
meant to be grafted upon this sacred vine in order to receive its fruitful substance and produce fruits of holiness.[34]
We are called to become the members of Jesus, our adorable Head, to live by His life and to be quickened by His
Spirit.

"We are here at the central point of the divine plan,"
writes Dom Marmion. "The grace of Christ, the Son of
God, is communicated to us to become in us the principle
of adoption. It is from this fullness of divine life and grace
of Jesus Christ that we must all draw. After having said
that the fullness of the divinity dwells corporally in Christ,
St. Paul adds immediately by way of conclusion: 'And in
Him who is the head of every principality and power you
have received of that fullness' (Col. 2:10)." [35]

Thus God's plan for us is realized: the vital union between the Head and the members which Jesus revealed to
His Apostles on the evening of Holy Thursday by means
of the following allegory. "I am the true vine, and My Father is the vine-dresser. . . . Abide in Me, and I in you.
As the branch cannot bear fruit of itself unless it remain on
the vine, so neither can you unless you abide in Me. I am
the vine, you are the branches." [36] Our spiritual life, there-

---

[33] *Ibid.,* 1:14.                    [34] Cf. John 15:4–5.
[35] *Christ the Life of the Soul,* First Conference, Part 5, p. 18.
[36] John 15: 1–4.

fore, must be a life in Jesus. Grace must continually flow from Him to us to make us bear fruits of holiness. "He who abides in Me, and I in Him, he bears much fruit; for without Me you can do nothing." [37]

Such is the law of our supernatural life: *Manete in Me!* Abide in Me! It is a union of faith and love, of will and action with the Son of God made man, an unceasing union with His sacred humanity. For, as St. Augustine tells us,[38] it is as man that Jesus is the mystical vine, whose branches we are. The life-giving union between Christ and His members permeates all their activities of soul and body, and without Him they can do *nothing.* Through this union they receive in a mysterious, hidden, but very real manner the purifying and life-giving influence of the sacred humanity of Christ, which makes them die with Him to sin and live in God.

The Incarnation is a mystery of love and mercy. It re-opened the source of all graces to the human race, corrupted through the sin of the first man. "But where the offense has abounded, grace has abounded yet more." [39] If the Word had not mercifully descended to our nature, we would not have been able to re-ascend to God nor to enter into a union of life with Him. How could we, the "children of wrath," [40] have aspired to become "members of God's household," [41] of whom St. Paul spoke to the Ephesians? The Incarnation has given us a divine Redeemer who wanted first of all to pay our debt and then to build a bridge between God and men by which we might return to the Father, to use one of St. Catherine of Siena's favorite images.[42] Thus, our Savior is truly our way to the Father,

---

[37] *Ibid.,* 15:5.    [38] Cf. *Commentary on St. John,* 15:1 ff.
[39] Rom. 5:20.    [40] Eph. 2:3.    [41] *Ibid.,* 2:19.
[42] Cf. *Dialogue,* Chapters 22, 26, 29, etc.

the light of truth that lights the road, and the life that
quickens us. "I am the way, and the truth, and the life." [43]

### TEXTS FOR MEDITATION

I am the true vine, and My Father is the vine-dresser. Every
branch in Me that bears no fruit He will take away; and every
branch that bears fruit He will cleanse, that it may bear more
fruit. . . .

Abide in Me, and I in you. As the branch cannot bear fruit
of itself unless it remain on the vine, so neither can you unless
you abide in Me. I am the vine, you are the branches. He who
abides in Me, and I in him, he bears much fruit; for without Me
you can do nothing.

If anyone does not abide in Me, he shall be cast outside as
the branch and wither; and they shall gather them up and cast
them into the fire, and they shall burn. If you abide in Me, and
if My words abide in you, ask whatever you will and it shall be
done to you. In this is My Father glorified, that you may bear
very much fruit, and become My disciples.

As the Father has loved Me, I also have loved you. Abide in
My love. If you keep My commandments you will abide in My
love, as I also have kept My Father's commandments, and abide
in His love. (John 15:1–10.)

I rejoice that the Holy Ghost is making you understand that
we have all things in Jesus Christ. For this knowledge is the
grain of mustard seed of which our Lord spoke. It is very tiny at
first, and when it is cultivated it becomes a great tree. Jesus
Christ is infinite Holiness: *Tu solus sanctus, Jesu Christe!* . . .
But not only is He holy Himself, He has also been given to us
to be our holiness: "Christ Jesus . . . has become for us God-
given wisdom, and justice, and sanctification, and redemption."
(I Cor. 1:30.)

He is our holiness:

[43] John 14:6.

First as our perfect model: "For those whom He has fore-known He has also predestined to become conformed to the image of His Son." (Rom. 8:29.) God finds all His joy in Him "This is My beloved Son, in whom I am well pleased." (Matt. 3:17.) And He is pleased in us in the mesaure that we resemble Jesus.

Secondly, as the means of union with God. In Jesus, divine and human nature are united in the unity of the Person, and we are united to the divinity in proportion to our union with the sacred humanity. (A letter by Dom Marmion.)

Most holy and eternal Father, Your divine Son assures us that no one can know Him unless You Yourself draw him toward Him, and that none of those whom You give Him will be lost. I therefore beseech You, in the name of the love You have for Him and that He has for You, to give me and all whom I love to this blessed Son, even as You communicate Your essence to Him, so that, having been begotten in Your Word we may share in the eternal glory that He renders to You and thus be sanctified in You.

O Son, eternal and holy like Your Father, You have promised that when You were lifted up from the earth You would draw all things to Yourself. Draw me to Yourself, therefore, O Be-loved of my soul, so that, being nourished by You I may live by You as You live by Your Father.

Holy Ghost, who fecundated the Blessed Virgin Mary in order to accomplish the mystery of the Incarnation of the Word, come to me, O joy of my heart and strength of my soul! Make me fruitful, so that Christ may grow in me and so that through You the closest of unions may be realized between this blessed Savior and my poor soul afire with Your love." (Dom Pius de Hemptinne, *Carnet du bon Dieu*.)

# CHAPTER 3 🖋

# *In the Light of Theology*

OUR divine Savior, the Son of God made man, has appeared to us full of grace and of truth. Every one of us receives of His fullness, that is, by means of a supernatural truth that enlightens us and a divine life that sanctifies us. We are engrafted on the mystical vine which is Jesus in His sacred humanity, so that we may receive His life-giving influx. We are incorporated into Him, as members to their Head, so that in Him we may become children of God.

St. Augustine tells us: "We see in our Head the very source of all grace, which is poured forth into all His members according to their own individual capacity. The grace that makes us Christians from the inception of our faith is the same grace by which this [God-] man became Christ. Man is reborn by the Holy Ghost, just as Christ was born by the Holy Ghost." [1] The Doctor of Hippo here affirms an identity of grace between the Christian and Christ, as well as an identity of birth. The reason is that the grace of the hypostatic union which unites God and man in Christ, which unites the Word and His human nature, is the source and principle from which sanctifying grace pours forth into us. This same humanity of Christ becomes the proximate cause of all grace, of all sanctification in men.

[1] *De Praedestinatione Sanctorum*, no. 31.

Hence, Christ is the author of life, as the Prince of the Apostles expresses it.[2]

But how are we to conceive of this mystery of grace? How can the humanity of Christ, tangible and corporeal like our own, produce grace? How can His most holy soul, which is a creature, transmit to our souls the supernatural life that is essentially divine and makes us share in the life of God Himself? "This is a hard saying." [3] It would be easy for us to repeat the words of Jesus' listeners when He announced the mystery of the Eucharist to them at Capharnaum. Can grace, which implies assimilation to God and a participation in His nature, be produced by anyone but God? And does not the sacred humanity, even though it subsists in the Word, remain a creature and therefore utterly disproportionate to the work of God?

How shall we answer this objection? It is true that God alone can produce grace as its first cause and as its principal agent operating through His own power. The gift of grace is so sublime that no creature, not even the human nature of the Word, could communicate it as its author. For it belongs to grace to deify our souls and, as St. Thomas rightly teaches, "it is as necessary that God alone should deify, bestowing a sharing in the divine nature by a participated likeness, as it is impossible that anything but fire should enkindle." [4]

But if the sacred humanity of Christ cannot sanctify our souls by its own power as principal cause, it can do so as an instrument of the power and goodness of God. Like the sacraments, and much more eminently than all the sacraments, the human nature of Jesus became a principle of grace and sanctification through its union with God. We

[2] Cf. Acts 3:15.        [3] John 6:61.
[4] *Summa theol.*, Ia IIae, q.112, a.1.

can say in all truth, to make use of a very exact and theological expression of the French School of spirituality, that the sacred humanity is the first sacrament of all grace,[5] the universal and supreme sacrament from which all the others derive their efficacy.

The sacraments, being sensible and efficacious signs of grace, have received the power to effect what they signify by reason of their institution by the Savior, through the strength of His words and the power of His divine will. The water of baptism expresses the purification of the soul in a sensible manner, but it does so in the name of God, who is represented by His minister. This water is, as it were, the word of God, a symbolic word whose mysterious signification is specified by its sacramental form. Now, it belongs to the word of God to produce what it expresses. His word creates, and His commands are infallibly obeyed. "He spoke and they were made: He commanded and they were created." [6] And so the baptismal water produces the adopted sonship which it signifies, in accordance with the profound words Jesus spoke to Nicodemus: "Unless a man be born again of water and the Spirit, he cannot enter into the kingdom of God." [7]

But the sacraments simply prolong and in a certain sense reproduce the mystery of the Word Incarnate. The sacred humanity of the Word is itself the living and permanent sign of God's mercy, the ever-actual testimony of His ineffable goodness to us. All the states and all the actions of Christ's adorable humanity—His lowly birth in a stable, His apostolic journeys in search of His lost sheep, His condition of immolation on the tree of the Cross, as well as His glorious resurrection and His ascension into heaven—

[5] Cf. *Ibid.*, IIIa, q.48, a.6, c.; q.49, a.1, ad 3.    [6] Ps. 32:9.
[7] John 3:5.

speak out and proclaim before the Father and before men
this sanctifying and divinely efficacious will of the Word
made flesh on behalf of the poor sons of Adam. Christ's
humanity is the supreme sacrament of life.

Christ's sacred humanity, united in soul and in body to
the Word, through the least of its acts and the lowliest of
its operations produces grace and communicates life to
souls that unite themselves to it through faith and charity.
St. Thomas points out: "The sacraments . . . are employed as signs for man's sanctification. Consequently they
can be considered in three ways, and in each way it is fitting
for words to be added to the sensible signs. For in the first
place they can be considered in regard to the cause of
sanctification, which is the Word Incarnate, to whom the
sacraments have a certain conformity, in that the word is
joined to the sensible sign, just as in the mystery of the
Incarnation the Word of God is united to sensible flesh." [8]
Such is the sublime harmony of the divine mysteries as
seen by the penetrating mind of the Angelic Doctor.

The Gospel gives us many examples of the power of
Jesus' sacred humanity in operation, either in performing
miracles or in sanctifying souls. We see Jesus curing the
sick by the touch of His hand, giving sight to the blind by
His saliva, and raising the dead to life by the power of His
words. Perhaps the most remarkable incident of all, in this
connection, was the cure of the woman who had suffered
from a hemorrhage for twelve years. She slipped furtively
through the crowd and came up behind our Savior. Filled
with a lively faith, she touched the tassel of His cloak, saying to herself: "If I touch but His cloak I shall be saved." [9]

Jesus asked: "Who touched Me?" But His astonished
apostles answered: "Master, the crowds throng and press

[8] *Summa theol.* IIIa, q.60, a.6.          [9] Matt. 9:21.

upon Thee, and dost Thou say, 'Who touched Me?' " Jesus insisted: "Someone touched Me; for I perceived that power had gone forth from Me." [10]

It was not the material contact that mattered. How many of these Galileans had had this privilege without, alas, deriving much benefit from it! This is far too realistic and heart-rending a picture of the way we often approach the Guest of our tabernacles, without the lively and life-giving faith of the sick woman in this Gospel narrative. Enlightened by grace, she was able to establish beneficent and efficacious contact with the life-giving flesh of Jesus; and this earned for her not only the cure of her illness but the praise of Jesus: "Only one person in all this crowd pressing around Me has touched Me in truth." On another occasion, St. Luke remarks in a general way that "all the crowd were trying to touch Him, for power went forth from Him and healed all" (Luke 6:19).

What Jesus did on behalf of bodies, He accomplished just as easily for the salvation of souls. He proved it when He cured the paralytic with the words: "Son, thy sins are forgiven thee." [11] The Scribes were scandalized and thought within themselves: "Who can forgive sins, but only God?" Jesus, knowing their secret doubts, asked: "Why are you arguing these things in your hearts? Which is easier, to say to the paralytic, 'Thy sins are forgiven thee,' or to say, 'Arise, and take up thy pallet, and walk?' " [12] And at that very instant the paralytic rose to his feet, took up his pallet, and went forth in the sight of all, cured and forgiven.[13]

To remit sins is to give grace. Now Jesus communicated grace many times in a sensible manner. By His presence within the womb of Mary He sanctified St. John the Bap-

[10] Luke 8:45–46.          [11] Mark 2:5.
[12] *Ibid.*, 2:7–10.          [13] Cf. *ibid.*, 2:12.

tist. By the contact of His sacred feet He granted to Mary Magdalen the grace of interior purification. By breathing on His Apostles after His resurrection, He communicated to them the grace of the Holy Spirit and the power to remit sins. And many other times He sanctified through His sacred humanity the souls that approached Him with the right dispositions. We need only mention Zacchaeus and the good thief in this connection.

St. Paul gives fervent praise to this life-giving and sanctifying power of the Word Incarnate. He reveals to the Ephesians what he calls "the unfathomable riches of Christ." [14] Still writing to the Ephesians, he says: "God . . . brought us to life together with Christ." [15] To the Colossians, he declares: "For in Him dwells all the fullness of the Godhead bodily, and in Him . . . you have received of that fullness." [16] Through grace we are continually under the influence of Jesus, so that we no longer live of ourselves but Christ lives in us.[17]

Over and over again the great Apostle repeats to the faithful that Christ is our life and our holiness. To the Colossians: "When Christ, your life, shall appear, then you too will appear with Him in glory." [18] On another occasion he writes: "For me to live is Christ." [19] And what is this life? It is the life of our souls, which consists in knowledge and love, the life of faith and charity, the life which we begin here below in the obscurity of faith and which will some day be consummated in the glory that Jesus will share with us. As St. Paul says, it is through faith that Christ dwells in our hearts, and through charity that we are rooted and grounded in Him, so that we "may be able

---

[14] Eph. 3:8.
[15] *Ibid.*, 2:4–5.
[16] Col. 2:9–10.
[17] Cf. Gal. 2:20.
[18] Col. 3:4.
[19] Phil. 1:21.

to comprehend with all the saints what is the breadth and length and height and depth, and to know Christ's love which surpasses knowledge, in order that we may be filled unto all the fullness of God." [20]

The Council of Ephesus, in its condemnation of Nestorius, has defined and canonized the doctrine that the sacred humanity of Christ is the source of our divine life: "If anyone does not confess that the flesh of Christ is life-giving, as being the flesh of the Word who quickens all things, let him be anathema." [21] And St. Cyril, from whom the Council borrowed the formula for this dogmatic definition, compares the flesh of Christ united with the Godhead to iron plunged into fire. Just as iron, reddened by flame, receives the properties of fire, namely the power to illumine and to give heat, so the flesh of Christ, and in consequence His whole human nature, receives from its union with the Word the power to cure and to vivify, to sanctify and deify our souls.

More precisely and no less forcefully, St. Thomas teaches the same doctrine when he repeats insistently that the sacred humanity of Jesus is the conjoined instrument of the Godhead (in contrast to the sacraments, which are separated instruments). When we call His sacred humanity a conjoined instrument we mean it is an organ of the Godhead, united to the Word in the unity of the Person, in order to be constantly at the services of the Son of God in the work of sanctifying souls. Let us listen to the Angelic Doctor: "Since Christ's humanity is the instrument of the Godhead, . . . all Christ's actions and sufferings operate instrumentally in virtue of His Godhead for the salvation

[20] Eph. 3:19.
[21] Cf. Denzinger, *Enchiridion Symbolorum*, no. 123.

of men." [22] And immediately he adds: "Christ's Passion,
. . . in relation to the Godhead, . . . draws infinite power
from it." [23]

Father Emil Mersch, S.J., translates this thought as follows: "Subsisting not in itself but in the Word, flesh of
God, body of the Life, and soul of the eternal Light, the
humanity of Christ, by all its fibers and by all its acts,
becomes a principle of life, of light, and of divinization." [24]

Such are the general outlines of this doctrine which is so
fruitful, so rich, and so well suited to nourish the life of
our souls. Who can help being filled with unlimited trust
and intense love for the sacred humanity of our beloved
Savior? Moreover, the adorable and life-giving humanity of
Jesus is not far from us. On the contrary, it is in our very
midst, in the divine Eucharist, and we can turn to it at
every moment. More wonderful still, we have the happiness
of receiving it within ourselves and of fusing it with our
own substance through Holy Communion. It thus becomes
a leaven of holiness and a principle of ever more abundant
grace and life, as Jesus Himself has told us: "I came that
they may have life, and have it more abundantly." [25]

God grant that we may make use of this inestimable
treasure with ever-increasing fervor and trust. In our necessities, in our spiritual deficiencies, in our impotence, and in
our afflictions of every sort, let us turn with faith to this
throne of grace, as St. Paul calls it, to find the remedy for
all our ills, and the principle and the source of all virtue
and holiness: "Let us therefore draw near with confidence

[22] *Summa, theol.*, IIIa, q.48, a.6.     [23] *Ibid.*, IIIa, q.48, a.6, ad 1.
[24] *Morality and the Mystical Body*, English translation published by
P. J. Kenedy & Sons, 1939, p. 77.
[25] John 10:10.

to the throne of grace, that we may . . . find grace to help in time of need." [26]

For them I sanctify Myself, that they also may be sanctified in truth.

Yet not for these only do I pray, but for those also who through their word are to believe in Me, that all may be one, even as Thou, Father, in Me and I in Thee; that they also may be one in us, that the world may believe that Thou hast sent Me.

And the glory that Thou hast given Me, I have given to them, that they may be one, even as We are one: I in them and Thou in Me; that they may be perfected in unity, and that the world may know that Thou hast sent Me, and that Thou hast loved them even as Thou hast loved Me.

Father, I will that where I am, they also whom Thou hast given Me may be with Me; in order that they may behold My glory, which Thou hast given Me, because Thou hast loved Me before the creation of the world. . . .

And I have made known to them Thy name, and will make it known, in order that the love with which Thou hast loved Me may be in them, and I in them. (John 17:19–26.)

Even though our sins make us unworthy to have our prayers heard, the holiness of Jesus and the fervor with which He prays for us make His Father forget our unworthiness and no longer think of anyone but the One whom He has constituted as our Advocate.

Besides, through our baptism we have become members of Jesus Christ. In consequence of this union, our needs are in a certain respect the needs of Jesus Christ. We can ask for nothing that concerns either the salvation or the perfection of our souls, that we do not also ask for Jesus Christ Himself; for the

[26] Heb. 4:16.

honor and the glory of the members is the honor and the glory of the body. (Blessed Jean-Gabriel Perboyre, C.M.)

O my God, O Trinity whom I adore, help me to forget myself completely and to fix myself in You, motionless and tranquil, as if my soul were already in eternity . . .

O my beloved Christ, crucified through love, I want to be the spouse of Your heart; I want to cover You with glory, I want to love You . . . enough to die of it. But I am aware of my helplessness, and I ask You to clothe me with Yourself, to identify my soul with all the movements of Your soul, to submerge me, invade me, and substitute Yourself for me, so that my life may be only a reflection of Yours. Come within me as Adorer, Expiator, and Savior.

O eternal Word, Utterance of my God, I want to spend my life listening to You, I want to become completely docile so that I may learn all things from You. And then, through the nights, the voids, and in moments of helplessness, I want to look steadily at You and remain under Your great light. O my beloved Star, fascinate me so that I may never withdraw from Your radiance.

O consuming Fire, Spirit of love, come upon me, so that an incarnation of the Word may take place in my soul; so that I may be for Him an additional humanity in which He can renew His Mystery.

And You, O Father, bend down over Your poor little creature, and see in her only Beloved One in whom You are well pleased! (Sister Elizabeth of the Trinity, O.C.D.)

# CHAPTER 4 ✌

# *Communion With the*
# *Mysteries of Christ*

"ALL Christ's actions and sufferings operate instrumentally in virtue of His Godhead for the salvation of men." [1] This great theological principle formulated by St. Thomas dominates the whole doctrine of our vital union with the Word made flesh. It contains unlimited possibilities for devotion and it offers souls enlightened by faith infinite riches of grace.

In the light of this principle every action of the sacred humanity of Christ, even the smallest and most insignificant, becomes a source of holiness: a gesture, a sign, a look is a mystery of grace. The look of Jesus! Let us call to mind the look He gave Peter who had just denied Him during the night of Holy Thursday. It crushed the heart of the unfaithful apostle with regret and sorrow. And so, too, the breath of the risen Christ communicated grace of the Holy Spirit to the disciples who had withdrawn to the Cenacle. Even now, the slightest movement of His loving heart produces in well-disposed souls a radiation of grace and a raging fire of love.

[1] *Summa theol.*, IIIa, q. 48, a. 6.

The acts of the Word Incarnate have merited grace for us because the union between the sacred humanity and the Person of the Son of God conferred infinite value on these acts. The excellence of an act is measured by the dignity of the person who performs it. But beyond that, the actions of Jesus had and still retain the virtue of producing grace in our souls. They are in very truth sacraments of sanctification.

However, the sanctifying power of the actions and mysteries of Christ is applied to us only to the extent that we, through a lively faith, unite ourselves to these mysteries and commune spiritually with Christ living, acting, and suffering for us. We can see, therefore, how vastly important it is for Christians to be well informed concerning this fruitful doctrine and to know this mystery of Christ [2] full of grace and truth.

In the last chapter we stressed the general principle underlying the sanctifying power of the most sacred humanity. Now we shall apply this principle specifically to the principal mysteries of Christ the Redeemer. In this application, we shall follow the Angelic Doctor step by step in the Third part of his *Summa Theologica,* in which he constantly comes back to this essential dogma of our life in Christ.

Speaking of the circumcision of our Lord, St. Thomas teaches that "Christ . . . took upon Himself circumcision, . . . to accomplish a spiritual circumcision in us," [3] through the repression of our passions and our death to the old Adam. With regard to the baptism of Jesus, the holy Doctor tells us, following St. Ambrose: "Our Lord was baptized because He wished, not to be cleansed, but to cleanse the waters, that, being purified by the flesh of

[2] Cf. Eph. 3:4; Col. 1:26.    [3] *Summa theol.,* IIIa, q. 37, a. 1, ad 3.

Christ that knew no sin, they might have the power of baptism." [4] This power of baptism, conferred upon the waters by the flesh of Christ, is unquestionably, according to St. Thomas, an operative power that produces grace, a sanctifying power that flows from the sacred humanity. More precisely, this power is derived from the act of divine condescension by which our Savior willed to submit to the baptism of penance conferred by St. John.

Throughout his study of the life of Christ, St. Thomas applies the same general principle. Speaking of the temptation of our Lord in the desert, the holy Doctor writes these lines, which are so heartening to souls undergoing similar trials: "Christ wished to be tempted, first that He might strengthen us against temptations. Hence Gregory says: . . . 'It was not unworthy of our Redeemer to wish to be tempted, . . . in order that by His temptations He might conquer our temptations, just as by His death He overcame our death.' " [5] It is a great consolation to us in the struggle of our frailty against the spirit of evil to be able to call upon the divine strength by which Jesus, our merciful Savior conquered the devil. If we cling trustfully to our divine Redeemer we shall be victorious in the battle, for Christ will triumph within us.

But it is above all when he deals with the Passion of Christ that St. Thomas stresses the sanctifying power that resides in the actions of the sacred humanity of Jesus. "Christ's Passion, although corporeal, has yet a spiritual effect from the united Godhead, and therefore it secures its efficacy by spiritual contact, namely by faith and the sacraments of faith." [6]

We should carefully note this twofold spiritual contact

---

[4] *Ibid.*, IIIa, q. 39, a. 1.        [5] *Ibid.*, IIIa, q. 41, a. 1.

[6] *Ibid.*, IIIa, q. 48, a. 6, ad 2.

which, according to St. Thomas, we have with the sanctifying Christ. A holy and life-giving virtue resides in His sacred humanity, but to receive its influx we must come into contact with it, just as in the natural order we can make use of the power of an electric current only by establishing contact with its source. Now life-giving contact with our divine Savior is accomplished through the sacraments—through the Holy Eucharist, which gives us the very source of holiness, and through the other sacraments which pour His sanctifying power into our souls.

Yet this is not the only means by which we can commune with the grace of Christ. Faith also places us in contact with this universal source of life and holiness. When we cling with a lively faith to Jesus and to His life-giving mysteries, to His passion, death, and resurrection, we achieve a real spiritual communion, a communion of life with Jesus. It is a spiritual communion that consists not only in the desire for the Eucharist which is commonly designated by this name, but also in our union of faith with the sanctifying mysteries and actions of the life of Christ. It is a communion that we must strive to achieve more and more frequently and in a more prolonged and continuous fashion, until we can at last say with St. Paul: "It is now no longer I that live, but Christ lives in me." [7]

That is how the life of Jesus becomes spiritually our own, in the words of the Apostle: "For to me to live is Christ." [8] The soul becomes progressively transformed by virtues of the mysteries of our Lord into the likeness of Jesus. It becomes more and more Christian in the profound sense of the word, that is to say, it becomes the property of Christ, His replica, His living prolongation.

Let us continue our study of the doctrine of St. Thomas.

[7] Gal. 2:20.  [8] Phil. 1:21.

Concerning the death of Christ, the Angelic Doctor remarks
that once the soul of the Savior has been separated from
His body, His sacred humanity could no longer merit.
Nevertheless, even then it could produce grace through
efficient causality, because the body of Christ was still
united to the Person of the Word: "In this way Christ's
death cannot be the cause of our salvation by way of merit,
but only by ways of causality, that is to say, inasmuch as
the Godhead was not separated from Christ's flesh by
death; and therefore whatever befell Christ's flesh, even
when the soul was departed, was conducive to salvation in
virtue of the Godhead united." [9]

St. Thomas then goes on to explain in greater detail the
nature of this grace which comes to us through the death
of Jesus. He posits a general principle in this connection
that deserves our closest attention because of the various
applications which it has in the practice of our Christian
life. "The effect of any cause is properly judged according
to its resemblance to the cause. Consequently, since death
is a kind of privation of one's own life, the effect of Christ's
death is considered in relation to the removal of the obstacles to our salvation, and these are the death of the soul
and of the body. Hence, Christ's death is said to have destroyed in us both the death of the soul, caused by sin, according to Romans 4:25: *He was delivered up for our sins;*
and the death of the body, consisting in the separation of
the soul, according to I Corinthians 15:54: *Death is swal-
lowed up in victory.*" [10]

According to this principle of the Angelic Doctor, each
mystery of Jesus and each of the actions of His most sacred
humanity accomplish in us a similar grace and an analogous
effect. His death makes us die to sin; His life makes us live

[9] *Summa theol.*, IIIa, q.50, a.6, c.          [10] *Ibid.*

in God; His prayer inspires us to pray fervently; His divine patience enables us to support our afflictions with love. All of His operations and virtues produce in our souls operations and virtues like His own. The ineffable purity of Jesus purifies us, restoring to our flesh its submissiveness to the soul in the service of love; His humility abases and casts us down before the majesty of God; His meekness makes us meek; His goodness makes us kind and merciful toward our brothers.

Let us see how Father Bourgoing, a disciple of Bérulle,[11] applies St. Thomas' principle to the entire economy of our spiritual life. "Everything in the Son of God is holy and sanctifying; everything is efficacious and a perpetual source of grace for us. Each of His virtues is the cause of the same virtue in us, and it never ceases impressing itself upon well-disposed hearts. Just as the sun is always shining, penetrating, and operating, just as a balm continually pours forth its sweet fragrance, so Jesus is the true sun of our souls and the precious ointment poured out upon them. The holiness of Jesus sanctifies, His humility humbles, and His purity purifies. Thus His obedience . . . and all His other virtues are poured upon us and produce their effects within us."

And what of the burial of Christ? St. Paul tells us and St. Thomas reminds us that baptism has made us participate in a special way in the mystery of Christ's burial. "We were buried with Him by means of baptism into death." [12] Enlightened by this doctrine, how can we fail constantly to renew within us the grace of our baptism and to hide ourselves with our adored Christ in death and in the

[11] It should be apparent how similar the doctrine of Bérulle is to that of St. Thomas.

[12] Rom. 6:4.

silence of the tomb, dying to the world and quieting within us the voice of the senses and of nature so that we may live the life of Jesus hidden in God? "For you have died and your life is hidden with Christ in God." [13] This is the particular fruit of the Fourteenth Station of the Cross.

But Christ did not remain in the tomb. He died in order to rise again, and His resurrection has in turn become the principle of our resurrection, both spiritual and corporeal. His resurrection is the cause of our spiritual resurrection through the life of grace which Christ's glorious humanity has the power to produce in our souls. But His resurrection is also the cause of our future resurrection according to the flesh.

To convince us of this truth, St. Thomas invokes an axiom from philosophy, which is corroborated by revelation: "Whatever is first in any order, is the cause of all that comes after it. But Christ's resurrection was the first in the order of our resurrection. . . . Hence, Christ's resurrection must be the cause of ours; and this is what the Apostle says (I Cor. 15:20–21): 'Christ is risen from the dead, the first-fruits of them that sleep.' " [14]

St. Thomas makes a careful distinction between merit and efficient causality with respect to the resurrection of Jesus, just as he does for His death. After Jesus entered into glory by His triumph of Easter, He no longer merited any grace whatsoever for us; but His glorious mysteries remained an efficient cause of life and holiness for us. "Properly speaking, Christ's resurrection is not the meritorious cause, but the efficient and exemplary cause of resurrection. It is the efficient cause inasmuch as Christ's humanity, according to which He rose again, is as it were the instrument of His Godhead, and works by its power. . . . Therefore,

[13] Col. 3:3.                    [14] *Summa theol.*, IIIa, q. 56, a. 1.

just as all other things which Christ did and endured in His humanity are profitable to our salvation through the power of the Godhead, . . . so also is Christ's resurrection the efficient cause of ours, through the divine power whose office it is to quicken the dead." [15] The Angelic Doctor goes on to say explicitly: "And this power by its presence is in touch with all places and times, and such virtual contact suffices for its efficiency." [16]

Let us note carefully the universal virtual contact which St. Thomas attributes to the sacred humanity of Christ and even to past actions of His earthly life. Habitually, there is no contact of substances between Jesus and ourselves, except in a certain respect in the precious moments after sacramental Communion. But there can always be the contact of influence, a very real action of His humanity and of all the mysteries accomplished in His humanity upon our bodies and souls, upon the men of all the ages since His incarnation. Herein lies the influence of the sacred vine of which Jesus Himself has said: "He who abides in Me [under the dominion of My sanctifying power], and I in him [by the operative action of My grace], he bears much fruit." [17]

The Ascension is the culmination of the series of mysteries in the life of Jesus here on earth. Far from putting an end to the sanctifying action of Christ, it places Him at the right hand of the Father, always living to make intercession for us [18] and always ready to communicate to us the effects of His life and of His passion. The mystery of the Ascension also possesses its own proper grace and salutary efficacy. St. Thomas teaches us that "Christ's ascension is the cause of our salvation not by way of merit, but of effi-

---

[15] *Ibid.*, IIIa, q. 56, a. 1, ad 3.     [16] *Ibid.*
[17] John 15:5.     [18] Cf. Heb. 7:25.

ciency.[19] He goes on to say: "Christ's ascension is the direct
cause of our ascension, as by beginning it in Him who is
our Head, with whom the members must be united." [20]
Thus the Angelic Doctor brings us back to the central
dogma of our spiritual life: the doctrine of the Mystical
Body of Jesus Christ, which gives us the key to all the
sanctifying mysteries of Christ our Savior.

According to the constant teaching of St. Paul, we are
the members of the total Christ, of which Jesus constituted
Himself the Head through His sacred humanity. Now it is
impossible that the head and the members should not be
quickened by the same life for the head determines the
movements of all the members and directs the activity of
the whole body. Likewise Jesus, having incorporated us to
Himself in holy baptism, communicates His life to us and
gives the impulse to all our good movements. He inspires,
directs, sanctifies, and fecundates even our least actions, our
innermost thoughts and our most secret affections. In very
truth, we live by Christ.

But this present action of Jesus within us is dependent
upon His past activity. His current influence is conditioned
by the mysteries of His earthly life, whose grace He continues to transmit to us and whose sanctifying power he infuses into us. It is the mystical prolongation of the life and
the passion of our Savior in His faithful which makes it
possible for each one of us to say with the Apostle: "What
is lacking of the sufferings of Christ I fill up in my flesh
for His body, which is the Church." [21]

Yes, our poor earthly life, which is so insignificant in
human terms, becomes—through the faith and love that
unite us to Jesus—precious in the eyes of God, who finds in

---

[19] *Summa theol.,* IIIa, q.57, a.6, ad 1.                    [20] *Ibid.,* ad 2.
[21] Col. 1:24.

it the memory of His divine Son's love and sacrifice. As St. Paul says: "And the life that I now live in the flesh, I live in the faith of the Son of God, who loved me and gave Himself up for me." [22]

Christ gave Himself up for us; but we can also say that He gave Himself to us. He is all ours. He belongs to us totally, together with His merits, His virtues, His mysteries, and His holy works. He is truly Jesus, our God, as we say to Him in the Litany of the Holy Name. It is up to us to accept this ineffable gift and to appropriate this treasure of the Son of God, who was made flesh in order to dwell among us.

One day St. Mechthild recommends the needs of a particular soul to our Lord, and He answered: "Why would this person not be willing to receive what I am ready to give her? I gladly offer her the whole of My most holy and innocent life upon earth. Let her take this life and supplement what is lacking to her own."

St. Mechthild continued: "Since you are so happy to have us seize all that is Yours, I beg of You to tell me, O most sweet God, how we must go about it."

Our Lord told her: "Offer to God the Father all your desires, intentions, and prayers, united to Mine. This offering will rise up to God and be accepted as one with My own, just as when various aromatics are thrown together into a fire they produce a single pillar of smoke that rises straight to heaven. Every prayer that is offered in union with My prayer is truly accepted by the Father as the fragrance of a precious incense. While all prayers penetrate heaven, they do not have the same value if they are not united to Mine."

He went on to teach her the practice of uniting all her

[22] Gal. 2:20.

works to the works of His own divine life: "All your labors and actions should be accomplished in union with My labors and works. The works of man can be ennobled by this means, just as copper melted with gold loses its own nature and takes on the quality of the precious metal. The works of man, which are nothing in themselves, grow when they are united to Mine, and their worth is transformed. Let man therefore measure his movements, his energies, his sentiments, his thoughts, his words, and his whole life by Mine. Then his life will be rejuvenated and ennobled, just as a bird might find its youth again by flying from a damp and pestilential climate into a healthy, life-giving atmosphere." [23] It can truly be said of St. Mechthild that her whole life was filled with the practice of uniting her actions to those of Christ and that this was the outstanding mark of her holiness.[24]

Through union with Christ we become participants of His divine riches and even of His divine Sonship, as His beloved apostle has told us: "To as many as received Him He gave the power of becoming sons of God." [25] We thereby realize the Father's intentions of eternal predestination. As St. Paul tells us: "Those whom He has foreknown He has also predestined to become conformed to the image of His Son, that He should be the firstborn among many brethren." [26] That is why the prayer that this beloved Brother taught us is His own prayer, a filial prayer in which we call God "Our Father!" That is also why the

---

[23] Cf. *The Revelations of Mechthild of Magdeburg (1210–1297)* or *The Flowing Light of the Godhead*, translated by Lucy Menzies (London: Longmans, Green and Co., 1953).

[24] An analogous statement can be made concerning the life of St. Gertrude. Cf. her revelations as related in *The Herald of Divine Love*.

[25] John 1:12.                    [26] Rom. 8:29.

Father has sent into our hearts a filial Spirit, "the Spirit of His Son," [27] as St. Paul writes to the Galatians: "And because you are sons, God has sent the Spirit of His Son into our hearts, crying, 'Abba, Father.' " [28]

If only we knew this great Gift of God! [29] O that we may love the mystery of the Word Incarnate and become ever more aware of the great love [30] with which He has loved us, so that we may love Him in return with our whole strength, as He asks us to do,[31] thinking only of Him, working only for Him, seeking only Him, and living only by Him and for Him!

Then and only then shall we have the right to say with the Apostle: "For to me to live is Christ." [32] Then we shall unhesitatingly add, "and to die is gain." [33] For death will consummate our life-giving union with our divine Savior, whom we clasp here on earth only in the darkness of faith. In heaven we shall contemplate Him face to face, in the radiance of His glorified humanity through which, as through a pure crystal, the light of the Godhead shines forth, to be the life and the happiness of the elect forever. This is the hope expressed so beautifully by St. Thomas Aquinas in the hymn *Adoro Te:*

> Jesu! whom for the present veil'd I see,
> What I so thirst for, O vouchsafe to me:
> That I may see Thy countenance unfolding,
> And may be blest Thy glory in beholding.[34]

---

[27] Gal. 4:6.　　　　　　　　[28] *Ibid.*
[29] John 4:10.　　　　　　　 [30] Cf. Eph. 2:4.
[31] Cf. Luke 10:27.　　　　　 [32] Phil. 1:21.
[33] *Ibid.*

[34] English translation in *The Raccolta,* (New York: Benziger, 1952), no. 166.

### TEXTS FOR MEDITATION

I praise Thee, Father, Lord of heaven and earth, that Thou didst hide these things from the wise and prudent and didst reveal them to little ones. Yes Father, I praise Thee for such was Thy good pleasure. All things have been delivered to Me by My Father; and no one knows the Son except the Father; nor does anyone know the Father except the Son, and him to whom the Son chooses to reveal Him.

Come to Me, all you who labor and are burdened, and I will give you rest. Take My yoke upon you and learn from Me, for I am meek and humble of heart, and you will find rest for your souls. For My yoke is easy and My burden light. (Matt. 12:25–30.)

Let us ask to feel the influence of these admirable and divine virtues of Jesus and of the ways He put them into practice, and to have some participation in them. Let us beseech Him to extend the arm of His omnipotence to implant them within us. This will perhaps be more effective than if we strain too much to produce acts of virtue, although we must not omit such efforts altogether.

All the mysteries of Jesus Christ, His words, desires, thoughts, movements, and all His holy operations, both interior and exterior, in short, all that is in Him or that proceeds from Him, all these things send out their rays, have their influence, and produce their efforts in us, provided we look upon and contemplate them with a gaze full of respect, honor, and reverence; and they pour forth their particular graces and implant their own virtues without any other effort on our part and without any formal act of virtue. (Francis Bourgoing, Priest of the Oratory.)

O my divine Master, You have made holy use of my being and of every state of life. By your birth in time You rendered to Your Father in my name all the duties that I should have rendered to Him in my life, and You practiced all the acts and exercises that I should have practiced. May You be forever blessed for it! With my whole heart I consent and cleave to everything that You have done for me! Indeed, I ratify and approve of it with my whole will. I would like to sign this statement with the last drop of my blood. I would also like to ratify with my blood all that You have done for me in all the other states and actions of Your life, to make up for the faults You knew I would be guilty of in the various states and actions of my life. (St. John Eudes.)

# CHAPTER 5 ✒

# *Through the Theological Virtues*

"FOR to me to live is Christ." [1] We have said that this must be the program of every Christian life: to live for Christ, to live with Christ, to live in Christ, according to the formula that the Apostle never tired of repeating.[2] Life in Christ Jesus follows necessarily from the truths of faith and from the theological principles that we have been analyzing according to the teaching of the Angelic Doctor. It is the only logical attitude for the Christian who wants to prove himself worthy of the name and wants to live by his baptism and follow his supernatural vocation. "I . . . exhort you to walk in a manner worthy of the calling with which you were called." [3]

But how are we to realize this life in Christ in practice? What must we do so that the grace of the mysteries of Jesus Christ will penetrate us and gradually transform us to the likeness of the Son of God made man?

First of all, with a deep and living faith, we must contemplate our divine Savior in the adorable mysteries of His

---

[1] Phil. 1:21.    [2] Cf. Eph. 2:7, 8, 10, 13; 3:6, 21.
[3] Eph. 4:1.

life. We must cleave to these life-giving mysteries with the trust that the Apostle had in the unfathomable riches of Christ—an enlightened and luminous trust—and we must seek in each mystery, in each of Christ's actions, the grace that belongs to it and fills our various needs. Through an efficacious charity we must succeed in performing all our actions in union with Jesus and as a continuation of His divine life.

The theological virtues contain the great resources of the Christian life, and yet the faithful, and even religious, do not always grasp their incomparable value and efficacy. In any case, these virtues are the supreme means of translating into practice the doctrine of devotion to the life-giving humanity of Christ.

To contemplate Jesus in His divine mysteries, to see Him with the eyes of faith living among men and offering Himself to us as the exemplar of all the virtues and the model of all perfection: this must be the first act, or better still, the fundamental attitude of a life of union with Christ. To live in Jesus we must know him; and to know Him is already to live by His life, according to His own divine words: "Now this is everlasting life, that they may know Thee, the only true God, and Him whom Thou has sent, Jesus Christ." [4] And this eternal life begins here on earth through faith.

Faith is not just ordinary knowledge—cold, theoretical, and abstract; it is a cleaving to God, who is primordial Truth and the fullness of perfection. It is a cleaving of the mind, enlightened by a supernatural light and directed to its divine object by an effective movement of the will. Through faith we already possess, in an obscure manner, the substance of the divine realities that we hope to see

[4] John 17:3.

face to face in heaven. In the words of St. Paul, faith is
"the substance of things to be hoped for." [5] The ultimate
term and the primary object of faith is God in the Trinity
of Persons, in the mystery of His innermost life. But faith
is also directed to the humanity of Jesus, subsisting in the
Word, the sacred humanity which became for us the living
Sacrament of God, the means by which we can go to the
Father, and the means of bringing God's graces down
upon us. It is the mysterious ladder that Jacob saw [6] and
was later revealed by Jesus Himself to Nathanael,[7] by
which the angels of God and the souls of Christians are
lifted up to the Godhead.

The Christian must therefore be assiduous in his contemplation of the most sacred humanity of Jesus. Then the
Gospel will become for him the supreme book of the spiritual life, because it offers the most perfect exemplar of
holiness. When he has understood Christ and tasted the
mystery of the Incarnation, he will love to read and re-read
the Gospel, to meditate upon it, enjoy it, and nourish his
devotion with it. Even the smallest fact about the life of
Jesus, His slightest gesture and humblest action will take
on great value in his eyes.

To quote Dom Marmion: "When Christ Jesus worked in
the humble workshop at Nazareth, when He conversed
with men or sat at meat with His disciples—things appar-
ently so simple—His father looked upon Him and said:
'This is My beloved Son in whom I am well pleased.' [8] And
He added: 'Hear Him,' that is to say, contemplate Him in
order to imitate Him; He is your Model." [9]

Indeed, since the heavenly Father looked down with so

---

[5] Heb. 11:1.                    [6] Cf. Gen. 28:12.
[7] Cf. John 1:51.                [8] Matt. 3:17.
[9] *Christ the Life of the Soul,* p. 39.

much love upon even the smallest acts of His Son's sacred humanity, we, too, should find our supreme happiness in gazing upon our divine Savior. We must reach the point of never taking our eyes from Him, of seeing Him in all things and at every instant. We must have a holy obsession with Christ, as it were, after the example of St. Bernard who found joy in nothing but the sweet name of Jesus, and after the example of St. Paul who proclaimed: "We are fools for Christ." [10]

St. Thérèse of the Child Jesus admitted that after having derived benefit from various spiritual authors and especially from St. John of the Cross, she finally reached the point during her last years when only the New Testament could provide solid nourishment for her interior life. That is the normal law of souls. In the beginning they do not discover in the simple Gospel text all the doctrinal substance, all the life-giving strength that is hidden in it, but by degrees their growing love for Jesus makes them penetrate more and more deeply into the treasures of grace and doctrinal riches that the Gospel contains.

Thus, the first act of our life of union with Christ Jesus must be to look at Him and gaze with the soul's eye deep into His mysteries until we can say with St. Paul: "For I determined not to know anything among you, except Jesus Christ," [11] because all other knowledge is contained in this one science of life and holiness.

But the insight of faith immediately sets Christian hope in motion. Knowledge of Christ the Redeemer fills the soul with a vast trust in the sanctifying power of His mysteries, for the mysteries of Jesus are sacraments of life. If we assiduously contemplate His sacred humanity we shall cleave to its divine wounds and its holy operations with the ardent

[10] I Cor. 4:10.  [11] *Ibid.*, 2:2.

desire to draw from them the treasures of grace that they
hold for us.

It is above all through this trustful union with the operations of Christ's humanity that we commune spiritually
with His mysteries, live by His life, appropriate His virtues,
and become filled with His spirit. Bérulle describes our
life-giving union with Christ as follows: "We bind ourselves to Jesus as to the One who by His divinity is the
source of our being and who by His humanity is the link
between our being and God, the spirit of our spirit, the
life of our life. In this pursuit of Jesus, in this cleaving to
Jesus, in this deep and continual dependence upon Jesus,
we shall find our life, our repose, our strength, and all our
power of operation."

One of Bérulle's disciples further clarifies the nature of
this sanctifying union with Jesus: "It suffices to look at
Jesus and to contemplate His perfections and virtues. This
vision alone is capable of producing marvelous effects in
the soul, just as a mere look at the brazen serpent sufficed to
cure the serpent bite. For not only is everything about
Jesus holy, it is also sanctifying and of a nature to impress
itself upon souls that faithfully consider it with the right
dispositions. His humility makes us humble; His purity
purifies us; His poverty, His patience, and His meekness
implant themselves in those who contemplate them. This
can be accomplished even when we do not think of ourselves in any way, through the mere fact that we are con-
sidering these virtues in Jesus with esteem, admiration,
respect, love, and delight." [12]

This gaze upon Jesus which is capable of communicating
to us the virtues of the divine Savior is a look of faith filled

---

[12] Father Rigoleuc, cited by Henri Brémond, *Histoire littéraire du
sentiment religieux en France*, Volume III, p. 145.

with great trust. To look at Jesus in this way is to become aware of what He is for us, namely, our Savior, Holiness incarnate, *our* holiness. "Christ Jesus, who has become for us . . . sanctification." [13] The soul's gaze upon Jesus is deeply consoling, sanctifying, and life-giving. It is a look of faith and love, and above all a look of trust that immerses us in the depths of Jesus' soul through the openings of His divine wounds and especially through the door of His transpierced heart.

Unfortunately, instead of looking at Jesus and His mysteries, many souls look at themselves, hypnotize themselves by a never-ending contemplation of their own moral wretchedness, and as a result of this depressing sight, sink into the pit of despair. To be sure, we must at certain moments recognize our failings and our poverty, but only in order to give wings to our hope and fly into the infinite abyss of Jesus' mercy, into the shelter of His divine heart. How right are the words of Mireille Dupouey: "Let us not talk to God too much about our misery. . . . The real danger is not so much our misery as analyzing our misery and giving it too much importance. Let us stop looking at ourselves with anguish when we can look at Him with love." [14]

Jesus had made this same reproach to St. Gertrude concerning one of her nuns who had stayed away from Holy Communion out of respect: "What can I do? These good souls keep the bandage of their unworthiness so tightly wrapped around their eyes that they cannot see the tenderness of My fatherly heart." [15] Dom Marmion had learned this lesson: "The more miserable, weak, and unworthy I am to be heard, the more should I cover myself with the

[13] I Cor. 1:30.    [14] *Cahiers,* 1919–1921.
[15] *The Herald of Divine Love.*

merits of Jesus and, strong in the faith I have in them, I
should approach the throne of God, that infinite mercy of
my Father, trusting as firmly to be heard through Jesus as
He did *pro sua reverentia* (Heb. 5:7), when He said, 'I
know that Thou hearest Me always.' This is the true spirit
of adoption." [16]

The reason why we should have unlimited trust in Jesus
is that He is *Jesus,* the merciful Savior, who came from
heaven to save the wretched and to communicate His
divine riches to them. As He Himself has said: "I have
come to call sinners, not the just." [17] So we can understand
the trust of St. John of the Cross, who wrote somewhere:
"O God, You will not take away from me what You once
gave me through Your only Son Jesus Christ, in whom You
have given me all that I desire," and the trust of St. Thérèse
of Lisieux, who wrote: "O Jesus, I feel that if, against all
probability, You found a weaker soul than mine, You
would delight in heaping upon it even greater favors,
providing it abandoned itself with complete trust to Your
mercy." [18] Already at the age of sixteen she had a perfect
understanding of this doctrine of trust, for she was able at
that time to write with the assurance of an experienced
spiritual director: "What offends Jesus, what wounds Him
to the heart is lack of trust!" [19] And the sole source of this
unshakable trust is always union with Christ and with His
saving mysteries.

St. John Eudes writes: "When we see that we are desti-
tute of every good, of every virtue, of all power and capacity
to serve God, we are necessarily led to stop relying on our-

---

[16] Dom Thibaut, *Abbot Columba Marmion* pp. 69–70.
[17] Matt. 9:13.                          [18] Cf. *Autobiography.*
[19] *Lettres de Sainte Thérèse de l'Enfant-Jesus,* (Lisieux, 1948),
Letter 71.

selves or on anything that pertains to us and to come out of ourselves as out of a hell in order to retreat within Jesus as in our paradise where we shall find in abundance all that we lack in ourselves. And when we do this, we rely upon Him, we entrust ourselves to Him, as in the One who has been given to us by the eternal Father to be our Redeemer, our justice, our virtue, our sanctification, our treasure, our strength, our life, and our all. This is what Jesus exhorts us to do when He invites us so lovingly and forcefully to come to Him in a spirit of trust: 'Come to Me, all you who labor and are burdened, and I will give you rest.' " [20]

To depend upon Jesus, our life and our all: this is true union with the God-man, the principle of all good and of all holiness, the infallible foundation of all trust.

We have spoken of the faith that contemplates Jesus in all His divine mysteries and of the union of trust with the sacred humanity which is the source of eternal life. We must now talk of love, divine charity, which is "the fulfillment of the law" [21] and "the bond of perfection." [22]

The love of Jesus! Union with Jesus through an ardent charity! Can we fail to sense that this is the zenith of the life-giving union with the sacred humanity of our divine Savior? We have only to look at the great Apostle St. Paul, who saw Jesus in everything, who lived only by Jesus, and who was relentlessly pressed and pursued by the love of Jesus. "The love of Christ impels us." [23] At the source of all these mysteries of our Savior's life, and above all at the source of His divine passion, Paul saw love, the love of a God carried to the point of folly. "Christ . . . loved me and gave Himself up for me!" [24]

---

[20] *La Vie Chrétienne,* chap. 3, art. 3.
[22] Col. 3:14.       [23] II Cor. 5:14.
[21] Rom. 13:10.
[24] Gal. 2:20.

This love became for the Apostle a power of unlimited dynamism, capable of overcoming all obstacles and of conquering all enemies who might attempt to wrest him from the love of God. He confidently cried out: "Who shall separate us from the love of Christ? Shall tribulation, or distress, or persecution, or hunger, or nakedness, or danger, or the sword? . . . But in all these things we overcome because of Him who has loved us." [25]

Because of Him who has loved us! This is the great, the only leitmotif in the life of an apostle: to know that one is loved by Jesus and to love Him in return, in life and in death. This is the secret of the life and holiness of all the souls intimately united to God through Jesus. Dom Pius de Hemptinne rightly said: "When we feel we are loved, we love or at least learn to love. O Jesus, that is how You conquer our souls!" [26] And St. Thérèse of the Child Jesus had said before him: "Love attracts love. Mine reaches out to You, it wants to fill the abyss that draws it." [27]

But the love that impels the soul to Jesus, the love for this God-man, our Model, is an active love, a transforming love, a love that makes us reproduce within ourselves the traits of the divine Exemplar. The soul that had contemplated Jesus with a lively faith and has attached itself with unlimited trust to His sacred humanity is naturally impelled to imitate Jesus in its whole life, to accomplish its every act with Jesus and in Jesus, to consummate a union of life and action with Jesus.

And it is not merely a question of imitating the divine Model from the outside. The movement of Christian grace

[25] Rom. 8:35-37.
[26] Dom Thibaut's *A Disciple of Dom Marmion, Dom de Hemptinne.* (London: Sands & Co., 1935), p. 119.
[27] Cf. *Autobiography.*

and the impulsion of the Holy Ghost press the soul to lose itself in Jesus, to become mystically identified with Him in order to act in Him, to yield itself to Him totally in its very depths, so that He Himself may act within it, so that in all that it does and says Jesus speaks, lives, and works within it. "Christ lives in me.[28] Christ . . . speaks in me." [29]

To act in Christ implies a twofold movement of the soul. First, we must picture Jesus in a situation analogous to our own: Jesus working, conversing, walking, praying, preaching, healing, suffering, or dying for us. As we know, all these acts and states of Jesus' life have unlimited sanctifying value, by which they can communicate something of their perfection and holiness even to our most insignificant actions.

Secondly, we must yield ourselves up to Jesus so that He may deign to continue working, praying, and suffering within us in this "supplementary humanity" that we are offering Him. We unite our work with the work of Jesus in order to place our tasks and our efforts under the influence of His divine work. We pray, uniting ourselves through faith and a loving will to the holy prayer of Jesus, and open up our soul to the influence of the Savior's prayer. It is the prayer of Jesus Himself that passes through our soul and that we offer up in union with Him to the heavenly Father.

During times of suffering, which often threatens to submerge our soul, we think of the sorrowful Passion of Jesus who suffered for the salvation of the world. We remember that the divine Redeemer wants to continue this work of salvation in union with all the saintly souls that make up at their own expense what is lacking of His divine passion.[30]

[28] Gal. 2:20.     [29] II Cor. 13:3.     [30] Cf. Col. 1:24.

How deeply moving is this continuation of the Passion of Christ Jesus in certain of His privileged ones! We see them abandon themselves to Him to renew in their flesh the bloody scenes of the work of the Redemption. Their hands and feet are pierced with invisible nails and they bear the bloody stigmata of their Savior; their hearts are wounded by love and pour forth large quantities of blood in ineffable agony, in union with the redemptive effusions of the adorable heart of their God. Blessed sufferings and blessed wounds that are the faithful reproduction of the wounds and sufferings of Jesus!

What these heroic souls accomplish in a visible manner, all of us must reproduce spiritually. Every suffering of a Christian is a participation in the Passion of Jesus, a splinter of the true Cross. In this, as in all our actions, we must unite ourselves to Jesus, submit to the power of His sufferings, to the influence of His holy Passion, and, in the nakedness of faith, carry our cross, which is the cross of Jesus.

Sometimes this cross will take the form of a particularly painful interior desolation: disgust with spiritual things, lack of light, the sentiment of being abandoned by God. Our consolation, and the only consolation that will be within our reach, will then be to unite ourselves with Christ in His mysterious desolation in Gethsemani, when He said: "Father, if it is possible, let this cup pass away from Me; yet not as I will, but as Thou willest." [31] Or when He cried out on Golgotha: "My God, My God, why hast Thou forsaken Me?" [32]

Thus, in all situations, whether painful or consoling, we can live the life of Jesus and continue His actions. There will doubtless be cases in which we shall not be able to

[31] Matt. 26:39.                    [32] *Ibid.*, 27:46.

establish as close a bond between our actions and those of Jesus, but that does not matter. We are not here concerned with a resemblance that is primarily physical and material, but with a spiritual and mystical conformity, an interior likeness in the soul, through our intention.

We can find this point of spiritual contact with the works of Christ in all our activities. Everything that we do is or at least should be the fulfillment of God's holy will. During His mortal life Jesus had but one thought: to accomplish the will of His Father. As He Himself said: "I do always the things that are pleasing to Him." [33] The will of God was so dear to His heart that it was the food of His life: "My food is to do the will of Him who sent Me." [34]

This is truly the highest perfection. It is the life of union with God and with His Christ in what is most formal, deepest, and most universal here on earth. Our union with God is accomplished by charity, St. Thomas tells us, [35] and true charity finds its expression in the accomplishment of God's will as Jesus reveals it to us in His Father's name: "If anyone love Me, he will keep My word." [36] And again: "If you love Me, keep My commandments." [37] And with a growing insistence that shows how fundamental this doctrine is in our Savior's mind: "If you keep My commandments you will abide in My love, as I also have kept My Father's commandments, and abide in His love." [38]

In truth, our perfection, our holiness, and our spiritual life lie in the supernatural union of our will with the supremely right and perfect will of God. God directs all

---

[33] John 8:29.    [34] *Ibid.*, 4:34.
[35] *Summa theol.*, IIa IIae, q.44, a.1: "Now the end of the spiritual life is that man be united to God, and this union is effected by charity."
[36] John 14:23.    [37] *Ibid.*, 14:15.    [38] *Ibid.*, 15:10.

things to the excellent end that He has assigned to them,
namely, Himself, His glory, and His infinite perfection, as
communicated to each creature and reflected in it according to its capacity. To arrive at this goal, each being must
obey the impulse it receives from God Himself, and for us
rational creatures, endowed with intellect and will, this
impulse is His will as manifested through His divine pre-
cepts. To withdraw from the path of God's commandments
is to lose one's way, to withdraw from God, and to deprive
oneself of all goodness and all perfection. But to cleave to
the holy will of God is to do all things according to His
law, to move toward Him, to love Him, and to unite oneself to Him as perfectly as possible here on earth and to be
infallibly led by Him toward the union and eternal possession of Him in heaven.

Such is the theology of charity and of the obedience in
which it is manifested in all our acts. "If anyone love Me,
he will keep My word." [39] But to come back to our life of
union with Christ, we must constantly bear in mind that
in the present plan of Providence, in the divine economy of
the Incarnation, the sanctifying will of God is revealed
to us and is fulfilled in us through the soul of Christ and
through the human will of the Word made flesh. He is the
divine intermediary between the Father and His adopted
sons, "one Mediator between God and men, Himself man,
Christ Jesus." [40] The Father "chose us in Him [Christ] before the foundation of the world, that we should be holy
and without blemish in His sight." [41] And what is "the
mystery of His will according to His good pleasure?" [42]
This mystery, St. Paul tells us in words whose doctrinal
substance we shall never completely fathom, is "to re-
establish all things in Christ, both in the heavens and those

[39] John 14:23.         [40] I Tim. 2:5.         [41] Eph. 1:4.
[42] *Ibid.,* 1:9.

on the earth." [43] And the holy Apostle adds: Therein lies "the counsel of His [the Father's] will," [44] who accomplishes all things "to the praise of His glory," [45] according to an eternal plan. This will is that we be sanctified and that we become His children, reflections of His glory, and that all of these things should come about through Christ and in Christ, in whom "we have redemption through His blood." [46]

It is clear, therefore, that Jesus is the supreme Artisan of the Father's works among us. He knows God's plan for us. The Father reveals all His wishes to Jesus so that He may make them known to us. That is why the Father said to us when He revealed the glory of His Son to us on Tabor: "Hear Him!" [47]

This is our holiness: to hear Jesus, who teaches us by His words; to hear and contemplate Jesus as He teaches us by His example; to look at Jesus and imitate Him as He reveals to us by His whole life the law of our perfection.

To conclude, it is with Jesus and through Jesus that we shall accomplish the will of the Father. It is in union with Jesus and following in His footsteps, identified as it were with His human will, that we shall love to do in all things "the will of Him who sent Him," the most lovable will of our heavenly Father, the will whose fulfillment we pray for each day in the *Our Father*, on earth as it is in heaven. *Fiat voluntas tua!* And this word *fiat* can easily become, for a soul that lives in union with Jesus, the expression of its innermost attitude.

In all circumstances, whatever may happen to me and however hard it may be for me, *Fiat!* Be it done to me according to Your will! With Christ in His agony, when the chalice of the Passion is presented to me: *Fiat!* With Jesus,

[43] *Ibid.*, 1:10.     [44] *Ibid.*, 1:11.     [45] *Ibid.*, 1:12.
[46] *Ibid.*, 1:7.     [47] Luke 9:35.

through Jesus, and in Jesus, I embrace all the desires of my heavenly Father, for His glory and that of His Christ.[48]

This is perfect love, free from all danger of illusion. It is the union of our will with God's through Christ. Our whole life of prayer and all our efforts toward union with God must lead to this love. It is the touchstone of all genuine Christian life, of all sound asceticism and mysticism. "If you love Me, keep My commandments." And this charity, in turn, is the term and the soul of every work accomplished according to God: "The end of the commandment is charity." [49]

### TEXTS FOR MEDITATION

In Him we have assurance and confident access through faith in Him. . . . For this reason I bend my knees to the Father of our Lord Jesus Christ, from whom all fatherhood in heaven and on earth receives its name, that He may grant you from His glorious riches to be strengthened with power through His Spirit unto the progress of the inner man; and to have Christ dwelling through faith in your hearts, so that, being rooted and grounded in love, you may be able to comprehend with all the saints what is the breadth and length and height and depth, and to know Christ's love which surpasses knowledge, in order that you may be filled unto all the fullness of God. (Eph. 3: 12–19.)

You must take on a new life in Him in Christ, imitating His wayfaring life His exterior and earthly life, so that He may make you worthy of participating in it. . . .

The Son of God says in the Canticle of Canticles: "Open to

[48] Prayer of the end of the Canon of the Mass: "Through Him, and with Him, and in Him, be unto Thee, O God the Father almighty, in the unity of the Holy Ghost, all honor and glory, world without end. Amen."

[49] I Tim. 1:5.

Me!" And why? "For My head is full of dew, and My locks of the drops of the nights."

This is the dew that you must collect and that He wants to pour upon you if you open to Him. This dew consists in His actions, His sufferings, His agony and sweat of blood in the garden, that you must collect. This must be your occupation and your life. He has left you the example of His life so that you might gather up the dew that falls from His head and the graces that this dew contains, for these are the drops of the nights.

The holy Mother of God has been filled with this divine dew, for she was open to God alone. God was her whole life and her continual occupation. During the time she spent upon earth after the Ascension of her Son . . . she collected this dew in the holy places where Jesus had prayed, fasted, worked, watched, preached, suffered, and died. That was her whole life, and in imitation of her you must do the same and collect this dew with her. . . .

O my God and my all, may the course of Your life upon earth, its moments, periods, and states, be applied to me and to my needs! (Bérulle.)

Lord, give me Your heart as a house of refuge. Grant that at the hour of my death no other path may be open to me for my eternity except the path of Your heart.

Lord Jesus, may Your divinity bless me, may Your humanity comfort me, may Your tenderness warm me, and may Your love keep me!

Lord, bury me within You! Be my hope and my joy, high above me, raising me up toward You, sustaining life within me, nourishing and rejoicing my soul, and make it grow. Behind me, be the desire that impels me. In front of me, be the love that draws and caresses my soul. To the right of me, be the praise that makes all my actions perfect. To the left of me, be the golden support that upholds me in tribulations. Beneath my feet, be a firm foundation to support my soul!

O most merciful Jesus, I bless You! I beg of You to deign to make up for all my insufficiencies.

O most merciful Jesus, I love You! I beg of You to offer up to the Father in my name, in place of all my imperfections, the love of Your heart! (St. Mechthild.)

# CHAPTER 6 🖋

# *The Wellsprings of the Liturgy*

"ALWAYS bearing about in our body the dying of Jesus, so that the life also of Jesus may be made manifest in our bodily frame".[1] This is the essence of our vocation as baptized Christians. The one and only means of fulfilling this divine vocation, of succeeding in this supernatural undertaking, is to remain in contact with the sanctifying mysteries of Jesus through faith, hope, love. It must be a life-giving contact that will unite all our activities, sufferings, interior movements, and exterior demeanor with the actions, sufferings, and holy dispositions of the Son of God made man.

When we understand the Christian life in this way, we do not live it alone, individually, each one for himself. We have not been life to our own initiative and to our personal resources in our effort to live by Christ and in Christ, to die to ourselves and to transform ourselves into Him. Divine Wisdom has entrusted us to the motherly care of the Church, in order to teach us to become children of God and brothers of Christ. It is she, the mystical spouse of

[1] II Cor. 4:10.

Christ, our Mother in the order of grace, who will teach us
to come close to Jesus, to unite ourselves to His mysteries,
and to live by His life. To this end, she offers us the price-
less resources of the sacred liturgy.

Is not this life with Jesus the very essence of the liturgy?
Is it not the life of Christ glorifying God in His members
by a cult of perfect worship?

Dom Festugière writes: "All the efforts of the liturgy are
directed to the development of the life of Christ in the
souls of the faithful. Considered in terms of its psycholog-
ical and moral effects, the liturgy is defined as the authentic
method instituted by the Church for assimilating souls to
Jesus." [2]

The entire program of liturgical spirituality is contained
in this formula: "To make the Christian share, season after
season and almost day by day, the sentiments of Christ in
His diverse mysteries, and thus to make man live by the
life of God." [3]

Through the supernatural pedagogy of her liturgy, the
Church continually renews man in Christ. By encompas-
sing the whole course of our lives within the mystical web
of her Christian ceremonies, she makes the human lifetime
enter into the procession of the mystery of Christ, "the
same, yesterday, and today, yes, and forever." [4] In the words
of Dom Guéranger: "The ecclesiastical year . . . is neither
more nor less than the manifestation of Jesus Christ and
His mysteries in the Church and the faithful soul. It is the
divine cycle, in which all the works of God appear, each in
its turn: the seven days of creation, the pasch and pentecost of the Jewish people, the ineffable visit of the In-

[2] Dom Festugière, *La liturgie catholique*, p. 119.
[3] *Ibid.*, p. 147.                    [4] Heb. 13:8.

carnate Word, His sacrifice and His victory, the descent of the Holy Ghost." [5]

There is, therefore, perfect agreement between the essence of the Christian life and what the sacred liturgy accomplishes in the Church and in each of her members. In both cases there is life-giving and sanctifying union with Christ and with His mysteries. The last end of the liturgy is the glorification of the Most Blessed Trinity by a regenerated humanity. But it is precisely through its union with Christ the Savior that the new humanity glorifies God and offers Him perfect praise, and this union with Christ is at the heart of the unfolding of the liturgical ceremonies. As the restorer of Solesmes also writes: "[God] has made the liturgy to be the center of His working in men's souls. Is not the formation of Christ [6] within us the result of our uniting in His various mysteries, the joyful, the sorrowful, and the glorious? These mysteries of Jesus come into us, are incorporated into us, each year by the power of the special grace which the liturgy produces by communicating them to us." [7]

Our devotion to the life-giving humanity of Christ is related to the most authentic devotion of the Church. It joins the present-day liturgical movement that is striving to bring about a renewal within Christian souls by a more conscious return to what has always been the highest expression of the Church's life.

Christ lives in His Church through the continuing cycle of liturgical feasts. The liturgy is not simply a commemoration of the actions of Christ's life or an imitative evocation

---

[5] *The Liturgical Year,* translated from the French by Dom Laurence Shepherd (Dublin: James Duffy, 1883), pp. 11–12.

[6] Gal. 4:19.           [7] *Op. cit.,* p. 20.

of these same mysteries or a kind of sacred drama that
presents to the faithful the great and only reality that is
worthy of captivating their attention. There is more, in-
comparably more, to the liturgical celebration. There is
the grace of the mystery that acts in the Church on the occasion of each feast, through each repetition of the divine
rites. The liturgical life realizes precisely and in a privileged way the life-giving contact of which St. Thomas
speaks when he says that "all Christ's actions and sufferings
operate instrumentally in virtue of His Godhead for the
salvation of men." [8]

It is this fact that Pope Pius XII's Encyclical *Mediator
Dei* stresses so strongly: "The liturgical year . . . is not a
cold and lifeless representation of the events of the past, or
a simple and bare record of a former age. It is rather Christ
Himself who is ever living in His Church. Here He continues that journey of immense mercy which He lovingly
began in His mortal life, going about doing good with the
design of bringing men to know His mysteries and in a way
live by them." [9]

Then, speaking of the mysteries of Jesus, the source of
life for men, the Holy Father adds: "These mysteries are
ever present and active, not in a vague and uncertain way
as some modern writers hold, but in the way that Catholic
doctrine teaches us." [10] And he explains that this teaching
is that "they are shining examples of Christian perfection,
as well as sources of divine grace, due to the merits and
prayers of Christ; they still influence us because each mystery brings its own special grace for our salvation." [11]

[8] *Summa theol.*, IIIa, q.48, a.6.
[9] Vatican Library Translation, published by the National Catholic
Welfare Conference, Washington, D.C., p. 57.
[10] *Ibid.*                                    [11] *Ibid.*

Thanks to the vital influence of these mysteries, whose spirit is transmitted to us, the Christian is transformed into our Lord and attains to spiritual perfection. "Moreover, our holy Mother the Church, while proposing for our contemplation the mysteries of our Redeemer, asks in her prayers for those gifts which would give her children the greatest possible share in the spirit of these mysteries through the merits of Christ. By means of His inspiration and help and through the cooperation of our wills we can receive from Him living vitality as branches do from the tree and members from the head; thus slowly and laboriously we can transform ourselves 'unto the measure of the age of the fullness of Christ' (Eph. 4:13)." [12]

All of this teaching corroborates the doctrine of the great Bérulle, who said that "the mysteries of Christ are past with respect to their execution, but they are present with respect to their power. . . . The spirit, the state, the power, and the merit of the mystery are still present." Then, taking up each of the terms he had just listed, he adds: "The spirit of God through which this mystery was accomplished, the interior state of the external mystery, the efficacy of the power that makes this mystery living and operative, . . . the merit by which He won us for His Father, and even His delight in it . . . is still living and present to Jesus as of the present moment."

While Bérulle's theology is general in its scope, it can be applied most aptly to the liturgical life of the Church, each of whose manifestations has the power to actualize the virtual presence of Jesus and His mysteries in His Mystical Body.

The liturgy is therefore not a simple remembrance of the life and beneficence of Jesus, an abstract contempla-

[12] *Loc. cit.*

tion, or a sterile representation. It is a communion with the life of Jesus. Each of the Church's solemnities renews in her faithful the virtues and dispositions of the divine Savior and tightens the bonds of faith and love between the Head and members of the Mystical Body. It is a progressive incorporation of Christians in Christ Jesus, a constantly increasing effusion of His fullness of grace and a growing communication of the fruit proper to each of His mysteries.

This is the mystical presence which Jesus promised to His friends when He was about to leave them: "Behold, I am with you all days, even unto the consummation of the world." [13] He was not speaking merely of help from the outside, nor was He referring directly to His Eucharistic presence through His sacrament of love. In this supreme promise Jesus was speaking of his vital permanence in the midst of His Church, a living and life-giving presence that includes both His help and His sacramental presence, for the Eucharist, as we shall see later, is the supreme means by which Jesus lives among His own and quickens them with His own life.

Father H. Bars writes with regard to the liturgical life: "A single force sets the entire course of human events in motion and this force is not an idea; it is a being, a person, a presence. It is the pontifical presence of our Lord Jesus Christ, who died the death we die and who triumphed over death; who lives and reigns with His Father in the embrace of the Spirit. The soul that has grasped this center of liturgical prayer will never lose its way; it is orientated once and for all and is fixed in the order par excellence in which the whole body is organized." [14]

[13] Matt. 28:20.
[14] "Les attitudes spirituelles dans l'Office," in *La Vie Spirituelle*, February, 1947.

This life-giving presence, this sanctifying action of Christ
Jesus in His Church through the liturgy spiritually renews
in us the grace of all His mysteries. But there is a hierarchy
among these mysteries that the liturgy makes the faithful
relive. There is a convergence of the whole liturgical year
toward one mystery that dominates all the others, and this
is the mystery of Easter.

In the early Church, Easter was not merely a great feast;
it was the one and only solemnity of the Church. But in
order truly to understand the feast of Easter, we must see
it the way it was formerly envisaged, as joining in a single
celebration the two complementary mysteries of the redemptive task of Jesus Christ: His passion and His resurrection, His death and His life. Better still, to come back
to the very meaning of the word Easter (Pasch or Passover), we must think of it as a passage from death to life,
with its necessary complement in the ascension of Christ
and the descent of the Holy Ghost upon the Church.

As Dom Froger writes: "In the first centuries of the
Church there was really only one Christian feast: the feast
of Easter. It began on Good Friday, reached its culminating
point on Easter Sunday, and continued during the fifty
days of the Paschal Season, including the Ascension, and
coming to an end with Pentecost. This last-mentioned feast
did not have an octave, and was less a feast in its own right
than a replica of Easter and the conclusion of the great
seven-week Paschal Feast. That is how Christians annually
commemorated the death and resurrection of the Savior
and all the mysteries related to them." [15]

The Paschal liturgy focused the attention of the faithful
on the central point of St. Paul's spirituality: "For you have
died [with Christ] and your [new] life is hidden with Christ

[15] Article in *La Vie Spirituelle*, April, 1947.

in God." [16] To die with Christ to sin and to rise again with
Him in God: herein lies the twofold orientation of our
Christian life. These are the two poles of all true spirituality, and this death and this life in Jesus are the immediate fruit of the Paschal liturgy, of the passion and
resurrection of Christ.

The Church was aware, as was the Apostle, that "we
were buried with [Christ] by means of baptism into death,
in order that, just as Christ has arisen from the dead, . . .
so we also may walk in newness of life." [17] That is why she
had fixed the time for the administering of baptism during
the night of Holy Saturday, that "truly blessed night" that
the deacon sings of so triumphantly in the *Exsultet,* the
night that witnessed the passage from death to life, from
the shadows of the tomb to the light of the Resurrection.
As "the child of light," [18] the neophyte affirmed, by his
spiritual resurrection on such a great day, the permanence
in the Church of the great mystery of the risen Jesus and
its annual renewal in the members of His Mystical Body.

But why are we speaking of the past? The Paschal solemnity has not changed in essence. By the provisions of
her recent decree, *Dominicae Resurrectionis,*[19] the Church
has made it clear that she wants her faithful to be fully
cognizant of the Paschal mystery and of the promises of
their baptism, whose particular grace is the grace of death
with Christ and of life in God. We must become aware of
these things by a renewed faith, and awaken within ourselves, through the Paschal liturgy, the grace of our baptism in order to put off the old man and put on the new.[20]

[16] Col. 3:3.                              [17] Rom. 6:4.
[18] Cf. Eph. 5:9; I Thess. 5:5.
[19] Issued February 11, 1951. Cf. in this connection Father Bouyer's
*The Paschal Mystery* (Chicago: Regnery, 1950).
[20] Cf. Eph. 4:22–24.

in grace, and its first-fruits were revealed in Christ's resurrection." [30]

We can see the true grandeur of Providence, which unites in a vast symbolism, embracing the whole duration of time, the two great divine works, the one prefiguring the other, creation being the type of the regeneration of the world.

In order to keep the mystery of Christ's resurrection more perfectly related to Sunday, the Church has not hesitated to upset the Jewish calendar, even at the price of strife with portions of Asiatic Christianity. She has decreed that the Christian Easter would not be celebrated from year to year on various days of the week, as was the Jewish Passover, but that it would always be solemnized on Sunday, and on the particular Sunday that followed the fourteenth day of the March moon. [31]

Each Sunday of the year reproduces, with less solemnity but with the same thrill of holy joy and with analogous fruits of grace, the great event of the Redemption, the Paschal mystery of Christ's death and resurrection, of His appearances to His apostles, and of His manifestation to His Church. As Dom Hild tells us, "it is important to note how much the Fathers insist on the fact that Sunday is not only the day of Christ's resurrection, but also the day of His appearances. Truly it is a day that cannot dawn without bringing daylight [into men's souls], without communicating its light and heat. Sunday, like Easter, is a theophany [a visible manifestation of God]. Each Sunday Christ appears anew to the Church *in mysterio,* and He makes her participate in His resurrected life. Each Sunday

[30] Article in *La Vie Spirituelle,* April, 1947, p. 551.
[31] More precisely, the Sunday after the fourteenth day of Nisan, that is, after the full moon following the Spring equinox.

Christ will thus continue to visit His Church until the eternal Sunday of the Second Coming." [32]

The liturgy of Sunday is an intimate revelation of the risen Christ to His Church, to the souls that know how to gather up the fruits of this weekly feast by their life of prayer and meditation. This is truly the most precious grace that comes from the celebration of Sunday. And does not the Church seek to assure us of these benefits by freeing us from servile work on that day? Our rest honors God's own rest after the creation. It also enables us to honor God by a more complete act of worship, to recover our spiritual energies, and to rest in God. It is a rest of the heart that makes us remember St. Augustine's great words: "You have made us for Yourself, O God, and our hearts are restless until they rest in You!"

The celebrations of Sunday and of Easter are two central points of the liturgy that unite us ever more closely to Christ and to God, and communicate to us in increasing measure the graces of life that have their origin in the Savior and in His sanctifying mysteries.

However, the annual cycle of the feasts of our Lord has been enriched through the centuries. Without detriment to the feast that will always remain the Feast of feasts (*Solemnitas solemnitatum* [33]), it makes us commemorate and relive—from Christmas through the twenty-fourth Sunday after Pentecost—all the outstanding mysteries of the life of Christ, thus sanctifying all the seasons of the year and illuminating them by the progressive radiation of our Savior's grace. What vast riches there are for us in this

---

[32] Article in *Maison-Dieu,* 1947, p. 33. For the mysticism of Sunday, see this entire number of *Maison-Dieu,* as well as the April, 1947, number of *La Vie Spirituelle.*
[33] Cf. *Martyrology.*

Christian year! What incomparable superiority over the dull and colorless year of the poor pagans, or of our modern pagans, without faith of hope, "without God in the world!" [34]

The series of the saints' feasts, which complements the feasts of our Lord, helps us to live Christ and to appropriate the inexhaustible grace of His mysteries and virtues. Since the saints are all members of Christ by a very special right, they reveal Him to us each in his own way and help us to reproduce within ourselves a particular virtue of our Savior, one of the rays of the total holiness of Christ. Christ's wisdom shines forth in the apostles and doctors; His strength and generous love triumph in the martyrs; His purity is manifested in the virgins. St. Francis of Assisi repeats after the Apostle: "With Christ I am nailed to the cross." [35] St. Thomas Aquinas reminds us of "Christ Jesus, in whom are hidden all the treasures of wisdom and knowledge." [36] St. Francis de Sales says again our Savior's words: "Learn from Me, for I am meek and humble of heart." [37] And through the whole life of St. Vincent de Paul we seem to hear the anguished cry from the Heart of Jesus: "I have compassion on the crowd." [38]

Above all the saints shines the face of the Virgin Mary, so clement and sweet. The Church is so completely under her conquering charm that she cannot stop thinking of her and thus multiplies feasts in her honor throughout the year. The truth is that Mary is so close to Jesus that to meet her is to find Jesus, to be with her is to live by Jesus. "He that shall find me, shall find life." [39] Is she not the Mother of Christ, she who gives Jesus, who brings Him forth in our souls, who communicates His life, and whose mysteries are

[34] Eph. 2:12.　　[35] Gal. 2:19.　　[36] Col. 2:3.
[37] Matt. 11:29.　　[38] Mark 8:2.　　[39] Prov. 8:35.

inseparably entwined with the mysteries of the Savior? We
shall discuss our Blessed Lady at greater length, as indeed
we must, in later chapters of this book.

But the liturgy possesses, in addition to the annual cycle
of feasts and the weekly renewal of the Paschal mystery
each Sunday, the daily re-enactment of the divine drama of
the passion and glorification of Christ, the living memorial
of the one Sacrifice, which is the primary source of all
divine life in men's souls. In short, the liturgy possesses the
Eucharistic sacrifice, and this we shall consider in the following chapter.

### TEXTS FOR MEDITATION

I urge therefore, first of all, that supplications, prayers, inter-
cessions and thanksgivings be made for all men; for kings, and
for all in high positions, that we may lead a quiet and peaceful
life in all piety and worthy behavior. This is good and agreeable
in the sight of God our Savior, who wishes all men to be saved
and to come to the knowledge of the truth. For there is one God,
and one Mediator between God and men, Himself man, Christ
Jesus, who gave Himself a ransom for all. . . .

I wish, then, that the men pray everywhere, lifting up pure
hands, without wrath and contention. In like manner, I wish
women to be decently dressed, adorning themselves with modesty and dignity, not with braided hair or gold or pearls or ex-
pensive clothing, but with good works such as become women
professing godliness. (I Tim. 2:1–10.)

It is in the Holy Church that this divine Spirit [of grace and
prayers] resides. He descended toward her like an imperious
wind, even while He appeared under the significant emblem of
tongues of fire. Since then, He has made his dwelling in this
fortunate Spouse. He is the principle of her movements; He is
the one who determines what her requests, her prayers, and
her canticles of praise shall be, as well as her enthusiasms and

her sighs. And as a consequence, for over nineteen centuries she has never been silent, day or night; and her voice is always melodious, her words always touch the heart of her Spouse. . . .

The prayer of the Church is therefore the most pleasing to the ear and to the heart of God, and hence the most powerful. Blessed is he, therefore, who prays with the Church, who unites his own prayer with the prayer of this Bride, whom the Bridegroom loves and always hears! (Dom Guéranger.)

Almighty and eternal God, although I am the most unworthy of Your creatures, I come with confidence before the throne of Your grace. . . . Uniting myself to the love that burned in your only Son as He adored You and accomplished the work of our Redemption, I shall begin and conclude this sacrifice of praise with the desire to offer You a tribute of honor like the one ceaselessly offered to You by the most sacred humanity of Jesus and by the most Blessed Virgin Mary. Thus, it is on the divine and always efficacious power of the Heart of Jesus that I base all my hopes. It is in His name, in the name of all the angels and of all the saints of heaven and earth that I shall pray, for Your eternal glory and praise. (St. Gertrude.)

# CHAPTER 7 ✒

# *The Eucharistic Sacrifice*

THE sacred liturgy, as we have seen, is the Church's most efficacious means for living and for making her children live in communion with her adorable Head, placing their souls in contact with the sanctifying humanity of Christ so that they can draw joyfully from the fountains of the Savior. Pope Pius XII teaches in his Encyclical *Mediator Dei* that the culminating point and the heart of the Christian religion is the mystery of the Holy Eucharist.[1] Indeed, all the sanctifying rites instituted by our Lord or inaugurated by the Church converge toward the Eucharist and the Sacrifice of the Mass. Does not the celebration of all Christian feasts—and above all the Feast of Easter and the Sunday liturgy—culminate in the Sacrifice of the altar?

The Holy Sacrifice of the Mass must be the center of our devotion if we desire to live by Christ, to be united to His life-giving humanity, and to become like Him through this union. To give Christians an understanding of the Mass, to teach them to unite themselves in the Mass to Christ, the Priest and Victim, to awaken in them the desire to become one with Jesus in the Holy for the glory of the Father *by living their Mass* throughout the day and by

[1] English translation, p. 27.

integrating all their activities into the permanent and continually renewed immolation of Christ on the altar—to do all this is surely to correspond with the deepest intentions of the Heart of Jesus, who came among us so that we might have life through the mystery of His passion, death, and resurrection. To do this is to give the faithful the supreme means for carrying out the program laid down by St. Paul: "For you have died and your life is hidden with Christ in God." [2]

With these things in mind, we shall first explain the Mass as the sacrifice of Jesus. We shall then show how the Mass is also the sacrifice of the Church.

Holy Mass is the mystery of faith, whose depths theologians never tire of sounding under the guiding light of Holy Scripture and Tradition. It re-presents to us and puts into the hands of the Church the climactic act of Jesus' life: the sacrifice of the Cross. To attain some understanding of it, within the limit of our means, we shall study it under its twofold aspect: as the sacrifice of Christ and as the sacrifice of the Church united to Christ.

First of all, the Eucharistic celebration is the sacrifice of Christ Himself; it is not a new sacrifice distinct from the sacrifice of Calvary. The Mass is the same sacrifice as that of the Cross, presented anew to God in an unbloody form, under the aspect of a sacrament. We must thoroughly grasp this idea in order to understand what the Mass is, in order to incorporate our own lives into it, and to sacrifice our whole selves together with it.

The Mass is the sacrifice of the Cross. There are not two sacrifices of Jesus Christ; there is only one sacrifice, valid for all eternity. St. Paul's doctrine on this point is very clear and the Angelic Doctor reaffirms it without any

[2] Col. 3:3.

diminution. "For by one offering He [Christ] has perfected forever those who are sanctified." [3]

It was upon this principle that St. Thomas based his
theology of the Mass. Far from seeing in it something that
detracts from the nature and value of the Mass as a true
sacrifice, he found in it the key to the whole mystery.
Viewed in this light, the Mass becomes "the sacrament of
the Passion."

Two and a half centuries after St. Thomas, Protestants
appealed to the same doctrine of St. Paul concerning the
*one* sacrifice in order to reject the Mass and to deny that it
is a sacrifice. Their spirit of pride ran afoul of this mystery,
and not being able to fathom its divine depths, they re-
jected it. Such is the fate of all heresy, for it always proceeds from a self-sufficient and arrogant mind that seeks
to measure divine realities in terms of natural reason. And
yet, in anything that concerns the sacrifice of the altar, the
mind of the universal Church and the whole of Christian
tradition should have put the innovators on their guard
against a superficial and erroneous interpretation of St.
Paul.

St. Thomas, who was wise and humble enough to cling
to the teaching of the Fathers, did not strike the stumbling
block against which Luther and Calvin were wrecked. He
asked himself: How can the Mass be the sacrifice of Christ,
since Christ immolated Himself only once, whereas the
Mass is renewed each day? [4] Therein lies the whole problem. Difficult as it may seem, St. Thomas solved it with his
usual facility, by resorting to a text of the great Doctor of
Hippo: "The Sacrifice which is offered every day in the
Church is not distinct from that which Christ Himself

[3] Heb. 10:14.
[4] Cf. *Summa theol.*, IIIa, q. 22, a. 3, obj. 2; IIIa, 2. 83, a. 1, obj. 1.

offered, but is a commemoration thereof" [5] and its *sacramental* renewal. He then cited the beautiful text from St. Augustine which speaks of the Mass as "the daily sacrament of the oblation of Calvary." [6]

It is through the simple and yet profound concept of the Mass as "the sacrament of the oblation of Calvary that St. Thomas explained the nature of the Eucharistic sacrifice and safeguarded its identity with the *one* sacrifice of Jesus on the Cross. Let us develop his thought.

Sacraments, in the mind of St. Thomas, are sensible and efficacious signs of an invisible and supernatural reality. Thus, baptism signifies and effects the spiritual purification of the soul by means of corporeal ablution. The Eucharist as sacrament signifies and contains the reality of the body and blood of our Lord, under the species of bread and wine, for the nourishment of our souls. Extreme unction represents and effects the entrusting of the sick person into the hands of God, together with the graces of healing and forgiveness that this implies.

The Mass, the Eucharist as sacrifice, has its place in the same order of sacramental realities. In the eyes of God and of the Church, it represents the bloody immolation of Calvary by reason of the visible separation of the Eucharistic species. It is a sacramental representation which has the power of making the holy Victim of Calvary present on our altars and of making the immolation of the Cross a reality at each celebration. In the words of St. Thomas, the Mass is "the perfect sacrament of our Lord's passion, as containing Christ crucified." [7]

This explains the oneness of the sacrifice of Jesus and

[5] *Summa theol.,* IIIa, q.22, a.3, ad 2.
[6] *De Civitate Dei,* Book X, Chapter 20.
[7] *Summa theol.,* IIIa, q.73, a.5, ad 2.

the unlimited repetition of the Mass. There is no contradiction in the fact that the sacramental sign, the visible and exterior sacrament, is multiplied in time and space, whereas the thing contained in the sacrament (what the theologians call the *res sacramenti*) remains one and unchanged. Such is the case of the Eucharistic presence in its relation to the immolation of Christ at Mass, as the Angelic Doctor also points out.[8] The faithful receive the sacred Host in all the sanctuaries of the world, but it is the same Christ whom they receive everywhere and always. It is the same flesh of Jesus that they consume to nourish their souls:

> Whether one or thousands eat,
> All receive the selfsame meat,
> Nor the less for others leave.[9]

Likewise, on all the altars of the Church, the ministers of Christ renew the Eucharistic oblation from sunrise to sunset. The rite is repeated from hour to hour in every corner of the earth, but the sacrifice that it contains and offers to God is everywhere the same. Through the hands of His ministers, the same Jesus, Priest and Host, continues to offer up to the divine Father in heaven the one and only oblation that He made of Himself on one particular occasion outside the gates of Jerusalem on the evening of the great Friday.

It is a mystery of love that we must first of all adore in its divine depths. And yet our faith, inspired by love, seeks to have some understanding of it with which to nourish our devotion. And this understanding is to be found in the fundamental concept that St. Thomas borrowed from

[8] Cf. *ibid.*, IIIa, q. 83, a. 1, ad 1.

[9] Verses from the *Lauda, Sion,* sung at the Mass for the Feast of Corpus Christi.

the ancient Doctors and that the Council of Trent canonized in substance in its famous Twenty-second Session.[10]

The concept of the Eucharistic sacrifice of Jesus must,
however, be complemented by another essential notion,
one that is particularly important for the Christian life:
The Mass is not only the sacrifice of Christ; it is also the
sacrifice of the Church, united to Christ. Pope Pius XII
stresses this point of doctrine in his *Mediator Dei*. Jesus is
not alone to be immolated on our altars. With Him and
through Him, the Church offers herself in the same sacrifice. The whole Mystical Body, united with its sacred Head,
is both priest and host. The Church, sharing in the
priesthood of Jesus, offers up the divine sacrifice with Him
in her own name as well as in His. Moreover, the whole
Church, one with Him in His victim state, is offered on
the Eucharistic altar and forms a single Host with the immaculate Lamb.

Let us clarify each of these two aspects of the sacrifice of
the Mass: 1) together with Christ, the Church offers; 2)
together with Christ, the Church is offered. These implicit
truths of our faith are of the greatest importance to the
Christian life, which is the life of Christ Jesus in His members through the sacrament of His sacred humanity. We
can therefore understand the Supreme Pontiff's emphasis
on this teaching.

First of all, in the Mass the whole Church offers up the
sacred victim. In order to unite the Church to His oblation,
Jesus communicated His priestly power to His apostles on
Holy Thursday, with the words: "Do this in remembrance
of Me." As the ministers of Jesus, bishops and priests are

---

[10] For a more detailed explanation of this doctrine, the reader is
referred to Charles V. Heris, O.P., *The Mystery of Christ, Our Head,
Priest, and King* (Westminster: Newman Press, 1950).

the prolongation and extension of the one and only Priest. Christ speaks through their lips and acts through their will. On the altar, Jesus operates through His minister who is a living sacrament.

But the priest likewise represents the Church when he offers up the divine sacrifice. The whole Church, being a supernatural society, owes this homage of sacrifice to God, this perfect cult of worship instituted by Jesus. Speaking to His apostles after His resurrection, He said: "As the Father has sent Me, I also send you." [11] And the Council of Trent assures us that Christ instituted the divine rite of the Eucharistic offering "that He might leave to His beloved spouse the Church a visible sacrifice." [12] Therefore, when the priest mounts the altar steps, it is in the name of the whole Church, of all his brothers in the faith, that he offers to God the Victim of propitiation, the Host of praise, adoration, and thanksgiving.

Any Christian who participates in the divine Sacrifice with an awakened faith cannot fail to grasp that in union with the priest he shares in the great offering of Christ on the altar. Pope Pius XII tells us: "Moreover the rites and prayers of the Eucharistic Sacrifice signify and show no less clearly that the oblation of the Victim is made by the priests in company with the people. For not only does the sacred minister, after the oblation of the bread and wine when he turns to the people, say the significant prayer: 'Pray Brethren, that my sacrifice and yours may be acceptable to God the Father Almighty;' but also the prayers by which the divine Victim is offered to God are generally expressed in the plural number; and in these it is indicated

[11] John 20:21.
[12] *Canons and Degrees of the Council of Trent,* English translation by H. J. Schroeder, O.P. (St. Louis: B. Herder, 1941), p. 144.

more than once that the people also participate in this august Sacrifice inasmuch as they offer the same." [13]

Indeed, is not the whole human race indebted to God for countless benefits? Must it not acknowledge Him as the principle of its creation and the object of its ultimate happiness? [14] From the beginning of time, sacrifice has been the adequate expression of this gratitude and adoration. On the other hand, in the present economy of revealed religion, there is no other sacrifice than the "clean oblation" offered up to God from the East to the West in all the nations of the earth, as the prophet Malachias announced. [15] Thus, it is the whole regenerated human race which offers up to God the sacrifice of our altars, through the hands of the minister of Christ.

How could Jesus, the Head of the Mystical Body, offer the divine Sacrifice alone? How could His members, who live by His life and are quickened by His Spirit, fail to be united to Him in this solemn act of homage to God His Father? The Head cannot offer Himself without His members, and Christ cannot repudiate His Church nor separate Himself from His Mystical Body in the act of renewing His great sacrifice of praise and love.

After all, did not the Prince of the Apostles call Christians a "royal priesthood"? [16] The character of baptism which consecrates us to the worship of God is, according to the Angelic Doctor, [17] a configuration to Christ the Priest and a participation in His eternal priesthood. It is true— as Pope Pius XII has stated forcefully in *Mediator Dei*, against those who recently tried to renew the Protestant

---

[13] *Mediator Dei*, pp. 33–34.
[14] Cf. *Summa theol.*, IIa IIae, q.85, a.2.
[15] Cf. Mal. 1:11.  [16] I Pet. 2:9.
[17] Cf. *Summa theol.*, IIIa, q.63, a.3.

doctrine—that this baptismal character does not elevate the ordinary faithful to the rank of ministers of Jesus Christ. They may not, as heads, preside over the Churches' liturgy, nor offer the holy sacrifice of the altar by themselves. In other words, they do not have the power to consecrate the bread and the wine, to change them into the body and blood of Christ, to elevate the Host and the chalice before God, and distribute them to their brothers. But they can, and by virtue of their baptism they *must,* unite themselves with the priest, unite themselves with Christ in the cult of adoration, love, reparation, and petition which He offers up in the name of all His "brothers" to God His Father through the Holy Sacrifice.

Now, if the whole Church is united to her divine Head in offering up the Sacrifice of the Mass, it follows that she is equally united to Him in His role of Victim. The Church, like Christ, belongs wholly to God and is consecrated to His glory. Jesus is as once Pontiff and Victim; His minister must be both priest and host; and the whole Church, with each of her members, participates in the priesthood of Christ and in His victim state. The intimate union between the Spouse and her divine Bridegroom, the indissoluble unity of the Mystical Body by reason of which the universal priesthood of the Church exists, also demands that she share His condition as a victim and that she learn from her divine Head to immolate herself with Him. This is one of the consequences of her supernatural nobility.

To understand this, we need only remember that according to the teaching of St. Thomas the gifts presented by the priest at the altar are the visible sign of the invisible sacrifice, the expression of the gift that he makes of himself to the sovereign Creator. The vicarious value of gifts offered was commonly accepted by all antiquity, both Jewish and pagan. And this belief found expression in a deeply symbolic gesture, which has remained unchanged in our Mass. The priest or the person who presented the victim to be immolated extended his hand over it as if to identify himself with it and to offer himself spiritually as a sacrifice through the medium of the victim. We find this same gesture in the Mass when the priest spreads his hands over the offerings immediately before the Consecration.[18]

We likewise know that for many centuries the faithful themselves brought to the altar the bread and the wine destined for the sacrifice. One portion of their offerings was actually used for the Consecration, while the rest was intended for the maintenance of the priest, in conformity with St. Paul's command: "Do you not know that they who minister in the temple eat what comes from the temple, and that they who serve the altar, have their share with the altar?" [19] The offerings of the faithful gave more forceful expression to the truth that Christians offer themselves, together with the immolated Christ, in the sacrifice of the Mass.

This brings us back to the heart of our doctrine on life-giving union with our Savior's humanity. It is in union with Him that the faithful, His mystical members, sacrifice themselves and die to sin. But it is likewise in union with Him that they live by the life of God, that they become God's "property," His inalienable possession, participating in His holiness and living by His life.

To grasp this last point, we must attain to a deeper understanding of the meaning of sacrifice. We must realize that immolation is not the whole of sacrifice; that the death of the victim is not the goal of the sacred rite, but only

[18] Cf. the prayer *Hanc igitur*.      [19] I Cor. 9:13.

its first phase; that it is only a means for attaining to life
in God, to the consecration of the host which will have
become God's property. Through the sacrifice, the host is
first of all withdrawn from all human use, all profane use.
That is the meaning of immolation. Then the victim is
consumed by the divine fire, accepted by God, and in a
sense symbolically perfected by Him, so as to make it a
sacred thing, His inalienable property, a holy and inviola-
ble thing.

This is what St. Thomas implies more than once when
he explains the meaning and the etymology of the word
sacrifice. To sacrifice is *sacrum facere,* to make a thing
sacred.[20] Clarifying his thought, he says: "If a thing be offered to be destroyed in the worship of God, as though it
were being made into something holy, it is . . . a sacrifice." [21]

And yet, as we have already said, the true sacrifice that
is offered to God through the medium of inanimate victims
is man himself, the creature endowed with intellect and
will. It is man's heart and soul, his whole being that the
Lord wants to possess. God wants to rule over man by His
law, to live in him through His grace, to transform him
into Himself, and to sanctify and deify him. That is why
St. Thomas, following St. Augustine, teaches that the end
of sacrifice is perfect union with God,[22] a cleaving to God
in a community of life.[23]

This notion of sacrifice brings us to the very foundation
of the Christian life, the program for every soul that has
been baptized and incorporated into Christ: death and life,
life attained through death. When we offer ourselves with

[20] Cf. *Summa theol.,* IIa IIae, q. 85, a. 3, ad 3; q. 86, a. 1.
[21] *Ibid.,* IIa IIae, q. 86, a. 1.        [22] Cf. IIIa, q. 22, a. 2, c.
[23] Cf. IIIa, q. 48, a. 3, c.

Jesus in sacrifice upon the altar of the Church, we must die to the world and to ourselves. Alas, we do not understand this well enough! But thanks to this death we become God's property together with Jesus, and we are taken up into Him, to live by His life: a life hidden with Christ in God.[24]

Jesus has gone before us on this sacred road. By offering up His sacrifice on the altar of the Cross, He died to His earthly life and He went to the Father. Through His immolation, He died to the world; through His glorification He was taken up into God. The sacrifice of Jesus did not end on Calvary, but was consummated in His resurrection and glorious ascension. By passing through the fire of glory, Jesus became the eternal Host, eternally acceptable to His Father. While Jesus was holy from the beginning, by reason of the grace of His hypostatic union, St. Thomas tells us that His humanity acquired a new holiness through the oblation of the Cross, the holiness or consecration that is the attribute of the host after it has been offered and accepted.[25]

In the most solemn moment of the Canon of the Mass, the anamnesis,[26] which follows the Consecration, the liturgy calls to mind this essential union of the three mysteries of Christ which are really only one: "the blessed Passion . . . , and also His resurrection from hell and also His glorious ascension into heaven." And this does not happen by chance. All the most ancient anaphoras [27] include this threefold commemoration at this part of the Mass, because the Eucharistic sacrifice is the mystical and sacramental re-

---

[24] Cf. Col. 3:3.          [25] Cf. *Summa theol.*, IIIa, q. 22, a. 2, ad 3.

[26] *Anamnesis:* remembrance or commemoration of the mysteries of Jesus.

[27] *Anaphora* or offering, the Greek name for the Canon of the Mass.

newal of the mysteries of His death and of His glorification,
which Jesus commanded His apostles to repeat in His
memory.

Just as the Christian is united to Jesus in His immolation, he must also be united to Him in this new life in
God, into which Christ entered through the door of Calvary. Mass must be for the Christian an inspiration to holiness. It must now be clear that the Mass, the center of the
liturgy, is for us Christians the supreme means of union
with the life-giving humanity of Christ and the primary
source of the graces of life that flow from the humanity of
Jesus into the souls of the faithful.

It is of the utmost importance, therefore, that the faithful
understand the riches of the Mass, that they know how to
participate in the Mass, and that they learn to live by the
Mass. Priests today are making great efforts to teach the
faithful to participate in the Mass and to live by the Mass.
For too many Christians, a meaningless routine has killed
this vital Christian attitude toward the Mass.

Attendance at Mass is an essential act of the Christian
life. By requiring this sacred duty on Sundays and holy
days of obligation, the Church has simply emphasized a
basic duty of every Christian that derives from our incorporation in Christ through baptism. We are Christians in order to glorify God with Jesus, His beloved and only Son.
And it is above all in the Mass that the incarnate Son of
God glorifies God in the name of all His brothers and
praises Him "in the midst of the Church." [28]

But there are many ways of attending Mass. There is the
formalistic "going to Mass" of those who attend only to
salve their conscience, without entering into the spirit of
the sacrifice. While such action is not absolutely without

[28] Ps. 21:23.

fruit or devoid of merit, it makes for superficiality. It leaves one in the periphery of the Church and almost outside the current of grace that flows from the altar to quicken souls with the life of Christ.

Then there is the attendance of those who pray at Mass (and this is a sign of progress) but who pray individually, so to speak, for their own intentions, instead of praying the Mass, instead of participating in the prayer and adoration of Christ in the public and official prayer of the Church.

Finally, there is the participation in the Mass of those who unite themselves to Jesus, Priest and Victim, during the celebration of the Mass, who relive, in their recollected and adoring souls, the one great sacrifice of the Cross; who offer up the divine Lamb in union with the priest for the needs of the Church, for souls in danger, for the extension of the kingdom of God upon this earth, for the extermination of the powers of evil in the world, for the sanctification of the ministers of God, and for the triumph of the Church. These Christians offer themselves as victims with Jesus, yielding their bodies and souls to whatever God's good pleasure may will for them; renewing within themselves the grace of their baptism; and killing their old self, their passions and their evil tendencies, in union with the immolated and crucified Lamb so that they may live their newly-found lives in God through faith, hope, and generous love. This is what Pope Pius XII urges us to do: "Nor should Christians forget to offer themselves, their cares, their sorrows, their distress and their necessities in union with their divine Savior upon the Cross." [29]

This spirit of immolation and total orientation toward God is really the soul of the Holy Sacrifice. With these

[29] *Mediator Dei,* English translation, no. 104.

same dispositions, but in an infinitely superior degree, Jesus offered Himself and continues to offer Himself on the altar. In this same spirit the fervent Christian participates in the great act of the Mass with the deepest joy.

In practice, there are many ways of actualizing this union with the immolated Christ. We can follow the prayers of the Church, composed under the inspiration of the Holy Ghost. Unless there is a strong, grace-given attraction to pray differently, this is perhaps the best method to recommend. However, some prefer to go back to Calvary in thought, to unite themselves to Mary offering up her Son and offering herself with Him, or to meditate upon the Passion of Christ renewed upon the altar.

The essential point is not to become isolated in too narrow and too personal a devotion, but to answer Jesus' invitation to His apostles: "Do this in remembrance of Me." Once this is assured, it is always permissible for the soul to yield to the inspiration of grace and to adopt a given interior disposition or attitude which answers its needs and inclinations of the moment. As we can see from the case of St. Gertrude, such variations correspond to the changing conditions of the soul's spiritual life, as well as to the various inspirations offered through the liturgical year.

But it is not enough to attend Mass or even to participate in the Mass for the space of a half hour, at the start of the day. The Christian who has an understanding of the divine sacrifice will strive more and more to make the fruits of the Mass flow into all of his activities. In short, he will seek to live his Mass. What does "living one's Mass" mean? It means remaining united in heart and mind with the adorable Victim; it means accomplishing all one's actions in the spirit of a host, no longer for oneself but for God. It means acting, not for the natural motives of selfish self-interest which so often spoil our good works, but for God and His glory, in docility to His divine Spirit, guided and lifted up by His love. Continual death to self and life in God: herein is the whole idea of sacrifice, the whole reality of the Mass, and the essence of Christian perfection.

The will to live our Mass will find countless ways of expressing itself in practice: in the exercise of charity with its tenderness and self-sacrifice; in generous self-forgetfulness for the benefit of our brothers; in the exercise of the apostolate by example as well as by words; in the fulfillment of the duties of our state in life, even those that are lowly and enslaving; in the smiling performance of duty that is sometimes so meritorious, not to say heroic—as St. Thérèse of Lisieux has shown us: in the acceptance of trials of every kind, from the daily annoyances and involuntary bruises that a generous soul spontaneously offers to its immolated Head, to the crucifying sufferings that are the lot of so many: bodily pain, trials of soul, or persecutions and opposition from those around us. For the true Christian all these things become flour for the host and the matter of sacrifice, which prolong in Christ's members the immolation accomplished on the altar.

A priest who has worthily celebrated the divine sacrifice has thus constituted himself a victim with Jesus. The Christian who has participated in the Mass with an understanding of this mystery of love has made himself a host with Christ. He no longer belongs to himself; he is all God's having been offered up with the divine Victim upon the altar of the Church. He must never take himself back, nor trifle with God. From one Mass to the next, he must accomplish more completely, in extent and in depth, in quality and in universality, the offering of his whole being, which he has surrendered to God for His glory alone.

May the priestly Virgin, who is so perfectly united to her Son, the eternal Priest and the immaculate Victim, obtain for her children this deep understanding of the Mass, this practical manner of entering into the spirit of the divine sacrifice, in order that they may celebrate it and participate in it like victims that are "living, holy, pleasing to God." [30]

### TEXTS FOR MEDITATION

For I myself have received from the Lord (what I also delivered to you), that the Lord Jesus, on the night in which He was betrayed, took bread, and giving thanks broke, and said, "This is My body which shall be given up for you; do this in remembrance of Me."

In like manner also the cup, after He had supped, saying, "This cup is the new covenant in My blood; do this as often as you drink it, in remembrance of Me. For as often as you shall eat this bread and drink the cup, you proclaim the death of the Lord, until He comes."

Therefore, whoever eats this bread or drinks the cup of the Lord unworthily, will be guilty of the body and the blood of the Lord. But let a man prove himself, and so let him eat of that bread and drink of the cup; for he who eats and drinks unworthily, without distinguishing the body, eats and drinks judgment to himself. (I Cor. 11:23–29.)

If the Father has united me to Him [Christ] so completely, it is in order to be able to continue the work of the Redemption within me and to transform me into Jesus crucified. He wants my life to be a continuation of the sacrifice of the Cross, just as the Mass is, . . . so that Christ may continue to suffer in me for the glory of His Father.

It is very crucifying, but it is also the happiness, the fullness of peace, for it is the fullness of union and consequently the fullness of glory for Him. For me it is a foretaste of heaven, a

[30] Rom. 12:1.

painful heaven, it is true; but the more I suffer, the happier I am, for it seems to me that each suffering gives Him increased glory. (Marie Antoinette de Geuser.)

O Sovereign Priest and Pontiff, Jesus Christ, who offered Yourself to God Your Father as a pure and spotless host on the altar of the Cross for our sins, You who have given us Your flesh as food and Your blood as drink.

You who have made it possible for us to renew this mystery by the power of Your Holy Spirit when You said the words: Do this in remembrance of Me! . . .

I beseech you to teach me by this same divine Spirit to approach this divine mystery with the respect, the devotion, and the holy fear that are due to it. Grant that through Your grace I may learn to raise my faith and my reason, my heart, my thoughts, and my conversations to the height of this great mystery, for Your glory and the good of my soul. (Prayer before Mass, *Roman Missal.*)

# CHAPTER 8 ✍

# *The Bread of Life*

THE sacrifice of the altar unites us to the immolated Lamb in His state of death, and even more to His risen state, as He lives forever by the life of God in His glorified humanity, but our union with the divine Lamb and our participation in His sacrifice is consummated in Eucharistic Communion. Here not only is the Lamb of God offered to the heavenly Father, we also eat Him, and thus our union with the immolated humanity of Christ is perfected by an ineffable invention of divine mercy: the love feast in which the immolated Lamb becomes the Bread of Life, the food of souls. Thus the Sacrament of the altar presents itself to our faith as the supreme means of communing with the life-giving humanity of Christ. Through this contact that is both sacramental and spiritual and answers all the needs of body and soul, we can draw from Christ's sacred humanity the fullness of divine life that resides within it. How vastly this truth broadens our supernatural horizon!

The Host of our sacrifice has become the Bread of Life! This is what Jesus promised his astonished listeners in His memorable discourse in Capharnaum: "The bread of God is that which comes down from heaven and gives life to the world." [1] And this bread communicates to us the life

[1] John 6:33.

that the Son of God receives in the bosom of the Father: "As the living Father has sent Me, and as I live because of the Father, so he who eats Me, he also shall live because of Me." [2] Jesus thus makes us reach back to the wellspring of our supernatural life: the Father. He tells us how this life, which the Father gives the Son in His eternal generation and which the Son communicates to His sacred humanity by His Incarnation, is given to us in the Eucharistic repast.

Moreover, we can commune with this Bread of Life through faith, in a way that extends beyond the sacramental union. Jesus made this very clear in His discourse of the promise: "I am the Bread of Life. He who comes to Me shall not hunger, and he who believes in Me shall never thirst." [3] To receive Him through faith is also to be united to Him and to share the life that He possesses in fullness. "For this is the will of My Father who sent Me, that whoever beholds the Son, and believes in Him, shall have everlasting life." [4]

Ardent faith, therefore, can enable us to attain to a life-giving union with the Son of God made man. Indeed, it can be very fruitful for our devotion to consider Eucharistic Communion within the broader framework of our spiritual union to the sanctifying humanity of Christ. Jesus repeats in many different ways: "He who believes in the Son has everlasting life." [5] And again: "He who believes in Me, as the Scripture says, 'From within him there shall flow rivers of living water.'" [6]

At the same time, Jesus has willed to exceed this purely spiritual union through faith and to make the communion of life closer and more efficacious, to facilitate it and to

---

[2] *Ibid.*, 6:58.   [3] *Ibid.*, 6:35.   [4] *Ibid.*, 6:40.
[5] John 3:36; cf. also 11:25, 26, etc.   [6] *Ibid.*, 7:38.

bring it within the reach of sensible creatures, composed
of matter and spirit. That is why He has invited us to
visible and sacramental Communion with His flesh and
blood. In the desert the Israelites ate a visible bread that
God rained down from heaven. Jesus Himself is now our
manna, the true bread sent from heaven to sustain us on
our journey toward the promised land: "Your fathers ate
the manna in the desert and have died. This is the bread
that comes down from heaven, so that if anyone eat of it he
will not die. . . . Amen, Amen, I say to you, unless you
eat the flesh of your Son of man, and drink His blood, you
shall not have life in you." [7]

Jesus insisted so much upon the literal eating of His body
that his listeners were astonished and scandalized: "For My
flesh is food indeed, and My blood is drink indeed. He who
eats My flesh, and drinks My blood, abides in Me and I in
him." [8]

But this Bread of life is not simply the flesh of Jesus.
As we have pointed out, it is the Host of our sacrifice, the
immolated body of the Lamb. Jesus told us this in His
discourse at Capharnaum: "He who eats Me, he also shall
live because of Me." [9] Since Communion is so closely related to the sacrifice of Jesus, it unites us to the mysteries
of the passion and resurrection of Christ and communicates to us all their life-giving riches. During the Mass, in
the essential act of the Eucharistic sacrifice which sacramentally renews the immolation of Calvary, our Lord prepares and gives the bread of our souls. By choosing bread
and wine as the matter of the Sacrifice of the Mass and by
changing them into His body and blood offered on the altar
of the Cross, He has clearly revealed to us His loving purpose: to make of His Host the food of our souls and to give

[7] *Ibid.,* 6:49–54.        [8] *Ibid.,* 6:56–57.        [9] *Ibid.,* 6:58.

us life through the sacrifice of His sacred humanity. At the Eucharistic banquet we receive the Victim of Calvary as our food.

In the preceding chapter we said that when the faithful participate in the Mass they should offer themselves as victims and become one with Jesus in the Host. Now we see that Jesus gives Himself to us as a Host, in order better to communicate to us His dispositions as a Victim. He invites us to the sacrificial banquet that customarily terminates every sacrificial rite.

Even in the Old Testament, in the patriarchical economy of the Jews, most sacrifices terminated by a communion or eating of the flesh of the victims offered up. By giving to His faithful as their food the gifts that He had consecrated and accepted, God was in a way welcoming the faithful to His own table as a sign of reconciliation and love. Jesus preserved for our benefit—in a far more sublime manner—this eating of the flesh of the Victim who is none other than Himself, this Communion at the table of sacrifice. Did not St. Paul, in speaking of idolatrous sacrifices, oppose "the table of devils" and "the table of the Lord"? [10]

To understand the full meaning of Communion, we must realize that it is a sacrificial banquet. Is this sufficiently understood and are Christians reminded often enough of this truth which is so rich in practical consequences and fruits of grace? Dom Marmion stresses this aspect of our Communion when he says: "But we unite ourselves to Christ as He is. Now every Communion presupposes the Sacrifice of the altar, and consequently the immolation of the Cross. In the offering of Holy Mass, Christ associates us in His state of High Priest, and in Communion He causes us to participate in His condition

[10] I Cor. 10:21.

of Victim." [11] Referring to the Apostle's teaching, he continues: "All this, says St. Paul, is recalled to our minds by Communion: 'For as often as you shall eat this bread and drink the cup, you proclaim the death of the Lord, until He comes' (I Cor. 11:26). Jesus Christ gives Himself to us as food, but after having been first offered as Victim; Victim and food are, in the Eucharist, sacrifice and sacrament —two inseparable characters." [12]

If we start from this idea we shall have a better understanding of how the Eucharistic Host is our Bread of life. It is from our union with the immolated Lamb that abundance of life and riches of grace come to us through Holy Communion. From this union comes the radical change in our moral and spiritual being, our death to our natural selfishness and earthly appetites, and our transformation into the likeness of Jesus, in His humble meekness, His self-sacrifice, and love. Jesus Himself has told us that the fruit of His sacrament is to liberate us from our selfish interests and make us abide in Him: "He who eats My flesh, and drinks My blood, abides in Me and I in him." [13]

The primary and principal fruit of the Host, which contains all the others, is the transformation of the communicant into our Lord. "It is now no longer I that live, but Christ lives in me." [14] Dom Marmion expresses this transformation very well: "Do not let us forget that Christ is ever living, ever acting. In coming to us He unites our members to His own; He purifies, He uplifts, He sanctifies, He transforms, as it were, all our faculties, so that, to borrow the beautiful thought of an ancient author, we love God with the heart of Christ, we praise God with the life of Christ, we live by His life. The divine presence of

---

[11] *Christ the Life of the Soul*, p. 272.     [12] *Ibid.*
[13] John 6:57.                                  [14] Gal. 2:20.

Jesus and His sanctifying virtue penetrate our whole being, both body and soul, with all their powers, so intimately, that we become 'other Christs.' " [15]

This supernatural transformation through the Eucharist is above all the work of charity. Communion, as St. Thomas teaches, is the sacrament of love. The fruit that belongs to it in particular is divine charity,[16] and charity transforms the lover into the object loved.

"The coming of Christ in us," Dom Marmion says, "tends of its nature, to establish between His thoughts and ours, between His sentiments and our sentiments, between His will and our will, such an exchange, such a correspondence and similitude that we have no other thoughts, no other sentiments, no other desires than those of Christ: 'Have this mind in you which was also in Christ Jesus' (Phil. 2:5). And this through love. Love yields our will to Christ, and through it, all our being, all our energies; and because love thus yields up the whole man, it is the means of our supernatural transformation and growth. St. John has well said: 'He who abides in love abides in God, and God in him' (I John 4:16)." [17]

Love is also the source of the deep spiritual joy that is one of the fruits of Communion in fervent and recollected souls. In the words of St. Thomas: "The soul is spiritually nourished through the power of this Sacrament, by being spiritually gladdened and, as it were, inebriated with the sweetness of the divine goodness, according to Cant. 5:1: 'Eat, O friends, and drink, and be inebriated, my dearly beloved.' " [18] This is the joy that little Thérèse of Lisieux experienced on the day of her First Holy Communion: "That day our meeting was more than simple recognition;

---

[15] *Op. cit.,* p. 267.     [16] Cf.*Summa theol.,* IIIa, q. 79, a. 4.
[17] *Op. cit.,* pp. 265–266.     [18] *Summa theol.,* IIIa, q. 79, a. 1, ad 2.

it was perfect union. We were no longer two. Thérèse had disappeared like a drop of water lost in the immensity of the ocean; Jesus alone remained. . . . And then my joy became so intense, so deep, that it could not be restrained; tears of happiness welled up and overflowed. My companions were astonished. . . . And no one understood that all the joy of heaven had come down into one heart, and that heart—exiled, weak, and mortal—could not contain it without tears." [19]

This is not to say that the joy of Communion must always have the exuberance and intensity of which St. Thérèse speaks. Even her own Communions were not always accompanied by these manifestations of sentiment. After all, these things are very secondary by comparison with the essential fruit of the Bread of life, namely, the transformation of the soul through charity. And this transformation must be the ultimate result of a normal Eucharistic diet.

We use the phrase "Eucharistic diet" because we must avoid any idealistic view that would not coincide with the nature of the Sacrament. Notwithstanding the views expressed in certain pious works, it is not in God's plan that a single Communion or even several widely-spaced Communions should work a complete change in our souls and bring us at once to perfect holiness. The Eucharist has been given to us as a Bread of life, and it is of the nature of bread to be eaten often, just as it is of the nature of life to grow by slow degrees. While Jesus, the Word Incarnate, can give us perfect holiness through a single Communion, He has no intention of working miracles in the order of grace, in opposition to the order established by Providence.

[19] *Saint Thérèse of Lisieux, the Little Flower of Jesus* (New York: P. J. Kenedy & Sons, 1927), pp. 74–75.

Man spends many long years reaching his full physical stature. The same is true of his spiritual stature. To attain "to the mature measure of the fullness of Christ" [20] requires persistent effort, with the help of grace and the practice of an intense Eucharistic life.

Frequent and daily Communion for both adults and children is in accord with the generous intentions of our Lord's love and also with the wishes of the Church, especially in recent times. Holy Mother Church obliges us to receive Communion at least once a year, simply as a way of keeping her hold on those of her children who have not understood the "very great love" [21] of their Savior. Such infrequent Communion could never be more than a feeble minimum of Christian life.

Are we to imply that all who have been receiving Communion every day or even every Sunday for a certain length of time are saints? It should be true, and yet it is far from being the case. The reason is that the effects of the Holy Eucharist—death to self with the immolated Lamb and transformation into Christ—are conditioned by and proportionate to the dispositions we bring to the sacred banquet.

If, after receiving Communion for years, we are still mediocre in virtue, very far from attaining to the fullness of Jesus' life within us, let us not blame it on the divine Sacrament's lack of efficacy. Let us reproach ourselves for our lack of docility and generosity in surrendering ourselves totally to the sanctifying influences and the transforming power of the Bread of heaven.

To receive Communion fruitfully, to draw from the sacred banquet the fruits of life that it contains, Dom Marmion tells us that "there is a very important general

[20] Eph. 4:13.                    [21] *Ibid.*, 2:4.

disposition drawn from the nature of union, which serves admirably as an habitual preparation for our union with Jesus Christ and, above all, for the perfection of this union: it is the total gift, frequently renewed, of ourselves to Jesus Christ." [22]

We should meditate upon this advice to give ourselves totally to our Lord, and put it into practice. For it is of the essence of Christianity, if indeed it is true that to be a Christian is to belong totally to Christ. Dom Marmion goes on to explain what he means: "The more we remain in this essential disposition which baptism inaugurated [of death to sin and of life for God], the better is our remote preparation for receiving the abundance of Eucharistic grace. To remain attached to venial sin, to deliberate imperfections, to willful negligence, and premeditated infidelities, all of these things cannot fail to impede our Lord's action when He comes to us. If we desire the perfection of this union, we ought not to bargain with Christ for our heart's liberty nor reserve any place, however small, for creatures loved for their own sake. We should empty ourselves of self, disengage ourselves from creatures, aspire after the perfect coming of Christ's kingdom within us by the submission of all our being to His Gospel and to the action of His Spirit." [23]

And we should make careful note of the fact that it is not our weaknesses, our imperfections, and our sins that impede the action of the Eucharistic food within us. For all these things are the precise reasons why we need Jesus and need Communion. The great obstacle lies in our attachment to these sins, our will to remain so attached; it is our lack of generosity in giving ourselves. So essential is this disposition of total surrender to our life-giving union

[22] *Op. cit.,* p. 270.                      [23] *Loc. cit.*

with Jesus that we shall again quote Dom Marmion's force-ful words: "What is it that prevents Christ from identifying us perfectly with Himself when He comes to us? Do our infirmities of mind or body, the miseries inherent to our condition as exiles, the limitations of our human nature? Certainly not. These imperfections, or even faults that escape us and that we deplore and strive to destroy do not prevent the action of Christ. On the contrary, He comes to help us to overcome these faults and to support our weak-nesses patiently; for He is a compassionate High Priest who 'knoweth our frame, and remembereth that we are dust.' " . . .

"The things that hinder the perfection of union are the bad habits known and not repudiated, which, from want of generosity, we have not the courage to attack; voluntary attachment to ourselves or to creatures. Christ cannot make us share in the abundance of His grace as long as we do not labor, by watchfulness over ourselves and by mortification, to uproot these bad habits and break off these attach-ments." [24]

We need to understand the true nature of the sacraments. We sometimes emphasize their intrinsic efficacy (*ex opere operato*) so exclusively that we forget that their effects are upon human beings, endowed with intellect and will. We forget that they adapt themselves to the needs of the sub-ject that receives them and that they require him to accept the gift of God with all the fervent spontaneity of his faith and of his loving will. Hence, if our souls are inert and our wills indolent, if we do not open our souls to the Bride-groom, if we do not go forth to meet Him, as Jesus suggests ("Behold, the Bridegroom is coming, go forth to meet Him!" [25]), then the Lord will merely pass through us, with-

[24] *Op. cit.*, pp. 270–271.      [25] Matt. 25:6.

out pouring out the abundance of life, the riches of grace, and the fervor of love that our souls are in no state to assimilate. For God in His omnipotence does not work useless miracles.

Let us, therefore, go to Holy Communion; but let us bring to this sacrament of life a soul that is fully awake and fervent. Then the divine banquet will become for us a source of life and holiness and the principle of our progress and spiritual growth.

There is one disposition in particular that is in deepest harmony with this "sacrament of unity," as St. Thomas calls it, after St. Augustine. It is fraternal charity. Did not Jesus Himself counsel us to go and be reconciled with our brothers before approaching the altar? [26] And did not the sacrament of love have its inception in the immense love of Christ immolating Himself for men, to gather them all into the unity of His Mystical Body? That is why the Angelic Doctor tells us that the fruit proper to the Eucharist is the unity of the Mystical Body of Jesus Christ.[27] That is also St. Paul's doctrine: "Because the bread is one, we though many, are one body, all of us who partake of the one [consecrated] bread." [28] This unity of His members is the great desire of Jesus, and it was the object of His sublime prayer on the eve of His death: "That all may be one, even as Thou, Father, in Me and I in Thee; that they also may be one in Us." [29]

The conclusion is inescapable: "When we communicate we must do so with the whole Christ, that is to say, unite ourselves by charity with Christ in His physical being and with His members; we cannot separate these two. . . . This is why the least willful coldness, the least resentment

---

[26] Cf. Matt. 5:24.　　[27] Cf. *Summa theol.,* IIIa, q.82, a.9, ad 2 um.
[28] I Cor. 10:17.　　[29] John 17:21.

harbored in the soul toward our neighbor, form a great obstacle to the perfection of that union which our Lord wishes to have with us in the Eucharist." [30]

By nurturing our fraternal charity, Holy Communion enriches and develops the life of the whole Church in her most diverse activities. The multiple relationships among the members of the Mystical Body find in Holy Communion a grace of fruitfulness and supernatural ardor.

The sacrament of love will always be the fire in which the flame of self-sacrifice must be kindled, whether for ministerial tasks or works of charity, whether for the service of souls or the relief of bodily ills. In Holy Communion will be awakened the tender charity that goes out toward all suffering and rejoices in all good; the charity that St. Paul has described in his Epistle to the Romans: "Love one another with fraternal charity, anticipating one another with honor. Be not slothful in zeal, be fervent in spirit, serving the Lord, rejoicing in hope. Be patient in tribulation, persevering in prayer. Share the needs of the saints, practicing hospitality. Bless those who persecute you; bless and do not curse. Rejoice with those who rejoice; weep with those who weep. Be of one mind towards one another. Do not set your mind on high things but condescend to the lowly. Be not wise in your own conceits. To no man render evil for evil, but provide good things not only in the sight of God, but also in the sight of all men. If it be possible, as far as in you lies, be at peace with all men." [31] These are the fruits of the sacrament of unity. In the Acts of the Apostles, St. Luke shows us that these fruits had been given in such abundance in the first Christian community that all of its members were as one body and one soul.

[30] Dom Marmion, *op. cit.*, p. 271.     [31] Rom. 12:10–18.

The Bread of life does not limit its efficacy to the present life. Jesus has promised: "He who eats this bread shall live forever." [32] This is also the Church's prayer for the communicant at the moment she gives him the divine Bread: "May the body of our Lord Jesus Christ preserve thy soul to life everlasting." As Father Joret writes, "In heaven will be perfectly accomplished the communion that Jesus desired and for which He prayed to His Father after the institution of the Eucharist: 'I in them and Thou in Me; that they may be perfected in unity' (John 17:23)." [33] It was with a view to this perfect union, this fullness of life in heaven, that Jesus instituted His divine Sacrament of love. Thus, every Eucharistic Communion is essentially a viaticum, food for the journey toward our homeland, just as the manna of the Jews was their food in the desert to sustain them in their march toward the promised land.

And the Eucharistic union will have as its effect and ultimate fruition not only the life of the soul and the beatific vision, but also the life of the body. It deposits in our bodies the promise and, as it were, the seed of their future resurrection: "He who eats My flesh and drinks My blood, . . . I will raise him up on the last day." [34] In the sacrament of the altar we receive the glorious body of Jesus, the body that suffered death for us and triumphed over it on the morning of His resurrection. He rose from the dead for all of us, and when He gives us His body as our food, He gives us a pledge of our future immortality.

We can now see that the sacred humanity of Jesus present in the Host is the inexhaustible principle and source of life that prepares us for eternal beatitude. "O sacred ban-

[32] John 6:59.

[33] F. D. Joret, O.P., *Aux sources de l'eau vive* (Paris: Desclée de Brouwer, 1928), chapter 2.

[34] John 6:55.

quet, in which Christ is received, the memory of His passion is renewed, the mind is filled with grace, and a pledge of future glory is given to us!" [35]

The Eucharist is the supreme sacrament of life and the sacrament of union, of divine life through union with the sacred humanity of Jesus. The other sacraments, as St. Thomas points out, are dependent upon the Sacrament of the altar. Each of them unites us through faith, in its own particular way, to this universal source of grace which we receive directly through the sacred Host. Each of them is, in its own way, a communion with the life of Jesus, a fountain of life that springs from the Savior's open side to pour into our Christian souls, according to their diverse needs, the riches of grace that the sacred humanity of Christ contains in fullness. Redemptive grace seeps through the humble materiality of these sacraments into the soul united to the body.

Tertullian says in his terse style: "The flesh is washed so that the soul may also be purified; the flesh is anointed so that the soul may be consecrated; the flesh is signed with the sign of the Cross so that the soul may be fortified; the flesh receives the imposition of hands so that the soul may be enlightened by the Spirit; the flesh is nourished with the body and blood of Christ so that the soul may be fattened with God." [36]

Baptism and penance in particular present themselves to our faith as wellsprings of a life of unlimited fruitfulness. This is true of baptism because it is the beginning of our life in God. By incorporating us into Christ, it unlooses the current of grace. And penance continually renews us in holiness by retrieving the losses our weakness has caused in our supernatural life.

Baptism, as we have said, is our birth in Christ. It makes

[35] Cf. *Raccolta*, no. 180.          [36] *De resurrectione carnis*, chapter 8.

us children of God. But this divine sonship is given to us only through union with Christ, through our incorporation in the only-begotten Son of the Father. This incorporation is likewise the fruit of the Eucharist. But the Angelic Doctor explains that baptism includes the desire for the Host [37] and thereby gives us the first fruits of its grace. Baptism is a sacrament that is always in act within us and we must constantly reawaken and activate its sanctifying grace through faith. Indeed, the whole of the Christian life, this life of union with Christ who prays and acts within His mystical members, is the blossoming of our baptismal grace; it is the fruit of this divine seed. Those who understand and actualize this union with the sacred humanity of Jesus in their interior and exterior life are simply living their baptism with greater intensity.

Confirmation complements the grace of baptism. It is a new union with Christ, for it gives us His Spirit of fortitude to combat the powers of evil within us and outside of us: the world, the flesh, and the devil. St. Paul has taught us that the adopted sons must be quickened by the Spirit of the only-begotten Son [38] and that only those who are led by the Spirit of God are the sons of God.[39] The Spirit of light and love is the soul of the whole Mystical Body and dwells in each of the members of Christ in the state of grace to guarantee their permanent and habitual docility to the sanctifying action of the Head.

Every Christian who is truly aware of the gift of the Holy Ghost will delight in invoking Him trustfully, in faithfully obeying His secret inspirations, and in asking of Him the deep understanding of Christ that it is His mission to give to the Savior's disciples. "The Spirit of truth

---

[37] Cf. *Summa theol.* IIIa, q.73, a.3.          [38] Cf. Gal. 4:6.
[39] Cf. Rom. 8:14.

who proceeds from the Father, He will bear witness concerning Me." [40] "Make Thou to us the Father known; teach us the Eternal Son to own." [41]

Knowledge of the Son, this science of Christ which the Holy Ghost teaches, in infinitely more efficacious and life-giving than the teaching of human doctors. At the same time, it does not abolish human knowledge but raises it to a higher level and makes it truly a science of life.

The sacrament of penance, complemented in life's last moments by extreme unction, re-opens the current of divine life that mortal sin had shut off. It communicates to us the infinite reparation offered by Jesus in His holy Passion for our offenses against God's majesty. It also applies to us the merits of this Passion, thereby restoring divine life to our souls. [42]

This sacrament exercises its life-giving influence even in souls that are not dead to grace. Its import remains the same and it loses none of its power over the soul that is already united to Christ but wants to derive greater benefit from His expiation and from the purifying action of His divine blood. These divine merits can be applied to past mortal sins or to present venial sins. That is why the Church encourages frequent recourse to the sacrament of penance. However, the faithful must be vigilant lest routine lull their faith to sleep and thus cause them to lose much of the riches of life that communion with the Passion of Christ through the sacrament of penance can bring to their souls.

Extreme unction is also a communion with the life-giving humanity of Jesus, designed to restore to the sick

---

[40] John 15:26.
[41] Concluding verse of the hymn *Veni Creator Spiritus*.
[42] Cf. *Summa theol.* IIIa, q.84, a.5.

"perfect spiritual health," [43] in preparation for the entrance into heaven. It would seem that when the priest anoints the sick person's senses to remove the remnants of sin committed by each of them, the perfection of the holy operations of Christ in each of His senses is communicated and sacramentally applied to the corresponding organs of the sinner, to eliminate from them every trace of impurity and every vestige of misconduct.[44] Thus the prophet Eliseus resurrected the son of the Sunamitess by applying his mouth against the child's mouth, his eyes against the child's eyes, and his hands against the child's hands.[45]

Social life is equally subject to the sanctifying action of Jesus. The family is sanctified in Christ through marriage; ecclesiastical society is constituted and constantly renewed by the sacrament of orders. The sacrament of matrimony presides over the transmission of temporal life, while the sacrament of orders governs the communication of spiritual life. In both societies Christ the Redeemer is intimately present. He is present by His grace in the love that unites husband and wife, for He is the supreme Spouse of sanctified humanity. His presence is capable of completely permeating the married life that has begun with His blessing. Marriage is truly "the great sacrament" of which St. Paul speaks and one whose riches of Christian living are now being studied by a very timely and promising theology.[46]

Even more powerful is the sanctifying action of Jesus in the grace of holy orders, inasmuch as the priest, His min-

---

[43] *Ibid.*, IIIa, q.84, a.1, ad 1 um.

[44] Cf. *Révélations de sainte Mechtilde, Le Livre de la Grâce Spéciale* (Paris, 1921).

[45] Cf. IV Kings 4:32–35.

[46] Cf., among others, Léon Cristiani, *Ce Sacrement est grand;* Dom Massabki, *Le Sacrement de l'Amour.*

ister, is another Christ. For it is He, Christ, who baptizes through the priest, who consecrates through the priest, who absolves through the priest, who preaches, blesses, and officiates in the person of the priest. *Sacerdos alter Christus.* Can one conceive of a more intimate union, a more complete identification than that existing between Jesus and His minister? It follows that the minister of Jesus, His *alter ego,* must live this life-giving union with His sacred humanity even more perfectly than other Christians. We can only mention this subject in passing.[47]

The sacrament of orders, more than any of the other sacraments, leads us to the Eucharist, the supreme Sacrament of life, since the priesthood is primarily ordered to the Mass and since its action upon the Mystical Body through preaching and the apostolate depends upon its action on the physical body of Jesus Christ present under the species of bread of wine. St. Thomas teaches: "The sacrament of orders is directed to the sacrament of the Eucharist, which is the Sacrament of sacraments, as Dionysius says. . . . Hence the distinction of orders is derived from their relation to the Eucharist. For the power of orders is directed either to the consecration of the Eucharist itself or to some ministry in connection with this sacrament of the Eucharist." [48]

Through the priesthood, which is ordered to the Mass, all the other sacraments are orientated toward the Sacrament of the altar as the center of all life and holiness. The priest's great resource for uniting souls to Christ and com-

[47] The union between Christ and His priest, which is so dear to Bérulle, Olier, and St. Vincent de Paul, is the dominant theme of Father Jules Leo Grimal, S.M., in his work *With Jesus to the Priesthood,* translated by Gerald Shaunghnessy (Philadelphia: The Dolphin Press, 1932).

[48] *Supplement,* q. 37, a. 2.

municating His divine life to them—whether in the pulpit, in the confessional, or anywhere else—is to induce them to go to the Eucharistic banquet, to make them understand that the Host is the Bread of life, to distribute this divine food to them generously, and to make their Communions bear the fruits of life that the Church expects of them.

We can now see more clearly how these riches of grace and this superabundance of divine life flow into our souls through the medium of the sacraments, which enable us to ceaselessly renew our contact with the God-man. "We can no longer touch the fringe of His garment, as did the woman suffering the hemorrhage, but a power still goes out of Him that heals us. We can reach Him and touch Him in these signs, for through them passes all the virtue of His humanity which is the organ and instrument of His Godhead. In these very lowly signs, our faith encounters Christ; and Christ, whose grace has already inspired in our souls this movement that raises us toward Him, answers our faith by infusing into us the grace that, together with the water of baptism and the blood of the Eucharist, never ceases flowing from His side that was pierced on the Cross." [49]

## TEXTS FOR MEDITATION

The cup of blessing that we bless, is it not the sharing of the blood of Christ? And the bread that we break, is it not the partaking of the body of the Lord?

Because the bread is one, we though many, are one body, all of us who partake of one bread. Behold Israel according to the flesh, are not they who eat of the sacrifices partakers of the altar? . . . but I say that what the Gentiles sacrifice, "they sacrifice to devils and not to God"; and I would not have you

[49] Thomas Camelot, O.P., "Le baptême, sacrement de la foi," *La Vie Spirituelle,* June, 1947.

become associates of devils. You cannot drink the cup of the Lord and the cup of devils; you cannot be partakers of the table of the Lord and of the table of devils. (I Cor. 10:16–21.)

For as often as you shall eat this bread and drink the cup, you proclaim the death of the Lord, until He comes.

Therefore whoever eats this bread or drinks the cup of the Lord unworthily, will be guilty of the body and the blood of the Lord. But let a man prove himself, and so let him eat of that bread and drink of the cup; for he who eats and drinks unworthily, without distinguishing the body, eats and drinks judgment to himself. This is why many among you are infirm and weak, and many sleep. But if we judge ourselves, we should not thus be judged. But when we are judged, we are being chastised by the Lord that we may not be condemned with this world. (I Cor. 11:26–32.)

The Blessed Sacrament! . . . In it resides the fullness of divinity. . . . In it you possess all things in their plentitude. The Blessed Sacrament presents itself to my mind as the dwelling par excellence of the Most Blessed Trinity. It is through the Blessed Sacrament that we live a life of close friendship with the Three. . . .

We feel the need of remaining completely united to Christ, in order to take full advantage of this Host of perfect praise; for it is in Him alone that we are a holy priesthood with the power to offer up spiritual sacrifices pleasing to God through Jesus Christ. (Marie Antionette de Geuser.)

My Benigna, be the apostle of My love. Shout so that everyone will hear you. Tell how I hunger and thirst, how I yearn to be received by My creatures! I remain in My sacrament of love for their sake, and they pay so little attention to it! . . . My Benigna, go out and find Me some souls who will receive Holy Communion! . . .

You know what the sister stewardess does when the gardener

comes. She goes down to the garden with him to show him the trees to be pruned, planted, and rooted up, and all that he has to do. Then she goes back into the house and he starts to work. . . . That is what you must do through Holy Communion: simply open your mouth to let Me enter the garden of your heart. I know what needs to be done. (Benigna Consolata.)

O Thou who art so merciful, Thou hast quenched Thy disciples' thirst from Thy chalice filled with joy, which is the price of the Redemption of the whole world! For Thou hast given Thyself in this holy mystery, with the words: "Drink My blood and be confirmed in the faith!"

Deign this day to let me take part in Thy mystical repast, O Son of God! For I shall not betray Thy mystery to Thy enemies! I shall not give Thee a kiss like Judas! But I shall say to Thee, bearing witness to Thee with the thief: "Remember me, Lord, when Thou enterest into Thy kingdom!"

When I receive fire, I tremble lest I be consumed, like flax and like grass. O redoubtable mystery! O mercy of God! How can I, who am but slime of the earth, receive the body and blood of my God, and become immortal because of it! . . .

Lord, that I may be sanctified in soul and in body! That I may be enlightened! That I may be saved! That I may become Thy sanctuary through communion with Thy holy mysteries! That Thou mayest dwell in me with the Father and the Spirit, O Benefactor rich in mercy! (From the Greek Office of St. Cosmas.)

# CHAPTER 9

# Quickened by the Blood of the Lamb

THE supernatural life comes to us chiefly through the sacrifice of Jesus, through His bloody immolation on Calvary, which governs the whole economy of grace of redemption. And this sacrifice continues to be everpresent, sanctifying, and life-giving in the Mass.

But in the sacrifice of the divine Lamb, the Precious Blood played the principal role. It was by the shedding of His blood that the work of our salvation was accomplished, that Jesus became the victim for our sins and the cause of our sanctification. That is why Scripture extols the virtue of the blood of the Lamb and the Fathers never tire of singing of the fruitfulness and inestimable benefits of the Precious Blood.

Among the saints, the noble Dominican virgin, Catherine of Siena, seems to have penetrated more deeply than many others into the mystery of the blood of Christ. In her letters, in fact in all her writings, she sings with mystical rapture and lyricism of the unfathomable riches of the Blood that redeemed us, of the Blood that gives us life.

The blood of Jesus is "the price of our redemption"

and "the life of our souls." These two aspects must be distinguished in the cult of the Precious Blood, following Scripture and the Fathers. The first aspect, "the price of our redemption," is more easily grasped and has captured the attention of the faithful more than the other. In the present chapter we shall lay special stress on the second aspect of the Precious Blood, as "the life of our souls" and as the source of our divine life.

St. Thomas, whose sober and measured words carry so much weight, has dared to write with astonishing exclusiveness: "There is only one cause of man's holiness, viz., the blood of Christ." [1] Only one cause? Is that not an exaggeration? To understand the universality of the affirmation, we must remember our oft-repeated principle: In the present economy of salvation all grace comes to us through the sacred humanity of Christ, which first of all merited it and afterwards, as the conjoined instrument of the Godhead, gave it to us and produced it in our souls. Now, the sacred humanity of Jesus merited these graces of life and holiness for us by all the actions and the mysteries of His life, but chiefly by His passion. These same mysteries of life and suffering are still operating instrumentally today in the transmission of grace. [2]

The efficacy of the other mysteries of Jesus has been subordinated, by the will of God, to the supreme efficacy of His passion. For God wanted Christ the Redeemer to triumph by the Cross. *Regnavit a ligno Deus.* [3] But to speak of the Cross is to evoke the blood of Jesus. If, therefore, the efficacy of the Passion, as the Angelic Doctor tells us, ex-

---

[1] *Summa theol.,* IIIa, q.60, a.3, obj. 2.
[2] Cf. *Ibid.,* IIIa, q.48, a.6.
[3] From the Hymn *Vexilla Regis,* sung on Good Friday: "God reigned from a cross."

tends to all times and places,[4] then it is truly the Precious Blood of our meek Lamb which is the universal and only cause of all grace and the fruitful source of all divine life. There is nothing in the present order of our salvation that we do not receive through the life-giving influx of the Precious Blood of Jesus. "There is only one cause of man's holiness, viz., the blood of Christ."

These words of St. Thomas are really a transcription of St. Paul's words to the Hebrews: "For if the blood of goats and bulls and the sprinkled ashes of a heifer sanctify the unclean, . . . how much more will the blood of Christ, who through the Holy Spirit offered Himself unblemished unto God, cleanse your conscience from dead works to serve the living God?" [5]

The victims of the Old Law obtained for God's people a purely legal and external holiness: the right to unite with the assembly of the faithful and to participate with them in divine worship. The immaculate Lamb gives us an inward holiness through His blood and a participation in the life of God Himself that makes us "citizens with the saints and members of God's household," [6] adopted sons of the heavenly Father and brothers of Jesus, the only begotten Son.[7] As the great Apostle also says: "Jesus, . . . that He might sanctify the people by His blood, suffered outside the gate," [8] thus fulfilling the prefiguration of the ancient victims that were burned outside the camp but whose blood was carried by the high priest into the inner sanctuary.

St. Paul places the entire New Testament under the sign of blood. Even as the Old Covenant was sealed in the blood of sacrifices, so the New Covenant, with all its graces,

---

[4] Cf. *Summa theol.* IIIa, q.49, a.1, ad 3 um.     [5] Heb. 9:13–14.
[6] Eph. 2:19.     [7] Cf. Rom. 8:29; 8:17.     [8] Heb. 13:12.

was inaugurated in the Blood of Calvary.[9] Jesus entered
the sanctuary of heaven by virtue of His own blood,[10] and
through this same divine Blood we are confident we shall
enter in after Him for all eternity.[11] However, in just retri-
bution, the Blood of the sacred Victim will call down
terrible punishments on him "who has trodden under foot
the Son of God and has regarded as unclean the Blood of
the Covenant through which he was sanctified." [12]

St. Ignatius of Antioch, echoing the teaching of St. Paul,
gave enthusiastic expression to his love and burning thirst
for the Blood that gives life, in his letters to the faithful
of the primitive Church. To the Romans he writes: "I want
to drink the blood of Christ which is incorruptible charity
and eternal life." [13] To the Ephesians: "You are imitators
of God, recalled to life by the blood of God." [14] Writing
to the Christians of Philadelphia, he began with this
magnificent salutation: "Ignatius, also called Theophorus
[that is, God-bearer], to the Church of Philadelphia, which
exults in the Passion of our Lord and which I greet in
the blood of Jesus Christ." [15] In another letter, written to
the Church of Smyrna, he said: "I glorify Jesus Christ
[our] God, who has made you so wise, and who has
strengthened you in charity by the blood of Christ." [16] In
other admirable letters the holy bishop who was to die a
martyr, appealed to the blood of Christ as the source of
charity,[17] the principle of unity,[18] the object of our faith,
or the subject of our condemnation.[19]

[9] Cf. Heb. 9:18–22.        [10] Cf. Heb. 9:12.        [11] Cf. Heb. 10:19.
[12] Heb. 10:29.                [13] *Letter to the Romans*, 7:3.
[14] *Letter to the Ephesians*, 1:1.
[15] *Letter to the Philadelphians*, 1:1.
[16] *Letter to the Smyrnans*, 1:1.        [17] *Letter to the Traillians*, 8:1.
[18] *Letter to the Philadelphians*, 4:1.
[19] *Letter to the Smyrnans*, 6:1.

And even before this glorious martyr, St. Clement of Rome had exhorted the faithful of Corinth to the worship and love of the Precious Blood of Jesus: "Let us attentively contemplate the blood of Christ, and let us realize how precious it is to His Father. Having been shed for our salvation, it has infused into the entire world the grace of penance." [20]

St. Cyprian, in a terse sentence of his well-known sixty-third Epistle, expressed in two words the twofold fruit of the Precious Blood which is the price of our redemption and the source of life: "Through the blood of Christ, we have been redeemed and quickened." [21]

At about the same time, Tertullian made the following commentary on St. John's words: "This is He who came in water and in blood, Jesus Christ." [22] In his treatise on baptism he writes: "Christ came through the water and the blood, to be baptized in the water and glorified in the blood, so that He might make of us likewise those who are called by the water and chosen by the blood. This is the twofold baptism that He drew out for us from the wound in His pierced side, so that those who believe in His blood may be washed by the water, and that those who have been washed in the water may also drink His blood." [23]

In the following century, St. Ambrose wrote with still greater force and precision in his treatise on the Holy Ghost: "The Apostle said: 'They drank from the spiritual rock which followed them, and the rock was Christ.' Now, this does not refer to the divinity but to the humanity of Christ, which flooded the hearts of all people, tortured by thirst, with the river of His blood." [24] Later he writes:

[20] *Letter to the Corinthians*, 7:4.
[21] Epistle 63.
[22] I John 5:6.
[23] *De baptismo*, chapter 16.
[24] *De Sancto Spiritu*, Prol. 2.

"Christ drank the chalice which was His passion, to make satisfaction for your crimes, so that you might quench your thirst for worldly pleasures with the sacred potion of His blood." [25]

All these passages from the holy Fathers reveal the faith of the first centuries in the purifying and quickening virtue of the Precious Blood of Jesus.

Among the Doctors of the Middle Ages, St. Albert the Great seems to have placed greater emphasis than anyone else on the power of the adorable Blood as the principle of the supernatural life. He dwells on it with particular delight in his treatise on *The Venerable Sacrament of the Altar:* "According to Genesis,[26] the blood is the seat of the soul, the principle and the cause of life. That is why no one lives by the spirit of Christ who is not united to His most pure blood." [27]

St. Albert's reference to Genesis and the application he makes of it can orientate our faith toward the understanding of the life-giving efficacy of the Precious Blood of our Lord. It suggests to us the analogy on which, according to the plan of divine Wisdom, the vital action of the Immaculate Lamb is based.

The Sacred Book tells us on several occasions: "The life of the flesh is in the blood." [28] The blood maintains and renews the animal life of the whole organism, for the blood diffuses throughout the body the nutritive elements needed by the various organs for their restoration and development.

Similarly, in the Mystical Body the blood of Jesus quickens all the members of Christ, maintaining, renew-

[25] *Ibid.*, no. 161.                    [26] Cf. Gen. 9:4–5.
[27] Edition Borgnet, Vol. XXXVIII, pp. 294–295.
[28] Lev. 17:11; cf. also Lev. 17:14; 7:26.

ing, and increasing their vital energies, their grace and the supernatural virtues, until they attain their full development. St. Bonaventure makes this point clear in a sermon for the third Sunday after Epiphany: "The corporeal life of Christ is in the blood of Christ, and likewise our spiritual and eternal life is in the blood of Jesus Christ. 'He who drinks My blood abides in Me.' Is it surprising that our life is in the blood of Christ? We are members of His body, we are part of His flesh and of His bones." [29]

In this as in the whole economy of our sanctification, God has maintained a proportion between the order of nature and the order of grace. He has given to sensible things a spiritual power that befits them. The water that washes our bodies purifies our souls; the food that sustains our mortal life is changed into the Bread that gives eternal life.

It is above all in the mystery of the Word Incarnate that this divine economy is verified. Everything that the Son of God assumed in the unity of His Person has become for us, His brothers, a sign and a cause of grace and holiness. The sacred humanity in its totality, in all the mysteries of its life, in all its actions, and by each of its movements pours treasures of divine life into our souls.

As we have said, the blood of Jesus is the principle of His earthly life. This is proved by the fact that Jesus spoke of the shedding of His blood to mean the giving of His life. Is it surprising, therefore, that the blood of the immolated Lamb should have become the inexhaustible source of our divine life? Everything in the sacred humanity of Jesus concurs in this work of life. And yet the divine Blood has a special claim in exercising this vital and sanctifying influence on the Mystical Body. That is

[29] *Sermo 3, in dom. I post Epiph.*

why the cult of the Precious Blood is so emphatically a
life-giving and sanctifying devotion.

To repeat: every part of Christ's sacred humanity participates in its instrumental power for the sanctification
of souls. However, the blood of Christ has primacy in this
work. For, while each of the actions of Jesus' life con-
tributed to the work of our redemption, it is primarily by
His Passion and death that Jesus saved us. It is by the
shedding of His blood that He wrested us from the power
of darkness to make us children of light.[30] By shedding His
precious blood on Calvary, Jesus laid down His life and
brought death to sin. When He took back His divine blood
on Easter morning, He resurrected His sacred body and
restored our souls to life. "Jesus . . . was delivered up
for our sins, and rose again for our justification." [31]

Death and life; death to the things of this world and
life in God. As we have said earlier, these are the two
poles of the great sacrifice of Jesus Christ. By His death,
as St. Thomas tells us following St. Paul,[32] Jesus brought
death to sin; by His resurrection He restored divine life
to men's souls. However, both Christ's death and His
resurrection involved the action of the adorable Blood,
shed on Calvary and afterward reunited to His resurrected
body on Easter morning. This is the full mystery of the
Blood of the New Covenant, of the eternal covenant that
assures us of everlasting life.

Unfortunately, many souls are as ignorant of this gift of
God as was the Samaritan woman. "If thou didst know
the gift of God!" [33] Hence the importance of instructing
the faithful on this mystery of life contained in the blood
of Jesus and of teaching them the inexhaustible fruitful-

---

[30] Cf. Col. 1:12–13.                                    [31] Rom. 4:25.
[32] Cf. *Summa theol.*, IIIa, a.56, a.2.                 [33] John 4:10.

ness of this divine river. Father Faber has described this fruitfulness with ardent lyricism: "Every supernatural act is a growth of [the Precious Blood]. Everything that is holy on earth is either leaf, bud, blossom, or fruit of the Blood of Jesus. To its fountains God calls the sinner, that he may be lightened of his burdens. . . . But the saints are no less called by God to these invigorating streams. It is out of the Precious Blood that men draw martyrdoms, vocations, celibacies, austerities, heroic charities, and all the magnificent graces of high sanctity." [34]

The blood of Jesus is not only the source of life and holiness for individual souls, it is also the great treasure of the Mystical Body as a whole, the river of living water that irrigates the spiritual garden of the Church. From the blood of Jesus the supreme Pontiff draws the riches of the Church's indulgences. From His blood the bishops and priests constantly renew the reserves of divine life that they distribute to their flocks. In His blood, religious communities regain their first fervor and draw vitality that can resist the disintegrating trials of time and bring forth from century to century, within the enclosure of their mystical solitudes or in the vast vineyards entrusted to their apostolic labor, flowers of holiness and fruits of virtue.

Each morning, before he mounts the altar steps, the priest appeals to the God who renews his youth because he aspires to the chalice of the divine blood that will revive the fervor of his charity. The Church as a body also sighs for this spiritual renewal amid the convulsions of a chaotic world. Through the secret and penetrating voice of mystical souls, through the merit of their sufferings,

[34] Frederick William Faber, *The Precious Blood or the Price of our Salvation* (Baltimore: John Murphy), pp. 25–26.

their tears, and their blood, the Church prays for the triumph of God's cause, the general awakening of Christian souls, and a more abundant effusion of the riches of the Precious Blood.

This life-giving Blood gushed from the many wounds of Christ's adorable body during His passion. It is up to us now to discover the wellsprings of life in the wounds of the Son of God and to draw forth their riches for ourselves and for many others.

Fountains of life, opened in the mystery of the Circumcision, in which Jesus strips us of the flesh of sin, clothes us in innocence and purity, and teaches us to walk in the path of Christian childhood.

Fountains of life, opened in the crushing agony of our Redeemer, during which the drops of divine blood fell like a fruitful dew upon our earth, defiled by sin but destined to bring forth the most beautiful flowers of holiness.

Fountains of life, opened in the cruel scourging when the divine blood of our adorable Savior covered Him as with a scarlet garment, to obtain for our souls the incomparable adornment of divine grace.

Fountains of life, opened in the praetorium during the crowning with thorns, when our beloved King stood before us resplendent as with a crown of brilliant rubies formed by the adorable droplets of blood on His sacred head.

Fountains of life, opened on the way of the Cross, during which fruitful seeds of virtue were planted under each step the divine Lamb took and under the painful impact of His falls, as blood streamed from His wounded limbs.

Fountains of life, opened on the holy Mount of the crucifixion, when His hands and feet received the blows of a hammer and the gash of crudely forged nails; and when four bright red streams irrigated the four corners of the globe as if it were a new Eden, to bring forth fruits of holiness.

Fountain of life, the most adorable of them all, opened in the Savior's side by the soldier's lance after the *Consummatum est*, to bring forth from His divine heart the supreme proof of His vast love and the permanent pledge of His infinite munificence—the water that washes us in baptism and the blood that inebriates us in the sacred banquet of joy.

Blessed and delectable fountains, O wounds of the Son of God open for us forever! Those of us who are conscious of the gift of God can plunge into these wounds to rid ourselves of the defilement of sin and grow rich with the treasures of the supernatural life.

Come then, O souls, disillusioned with the world, come to these fountains of joy and you will regain your love for the life that knows no end. Come, souls crushed under the weight of trials, come to these fountains of spiritual strength. You will draw from them the courage to go on to the end of the sorrowful path that ends, beyond Calvary, in a life of glory. Come, souls defiled by a thousand sins and despairing of divine mercy. The blood that flows from our Savior's wounds washes away all turpitude. It transforms the lost woman of Magdala into St. Mary Magdalen, the odor of whose holiness fills the earth. And you above all, souls eager for life and holiness, come to the fountains from which life and holiness flow. You will draw from them the graces of secret prayer, the treasures of generous love, and you will be transformed by the virtue of the adorable blood into the Beloved who calls to you. Then you will be able to say with the great Apostle: "It is now no longer I that live, but Christ lives in me." [35]

Yes, let us all go toward these "fountains of the Savior" so that we may find the riches of life and grace that God has hidden in them, and let us repeat from our hearts the words of St. Thérèse of the Child Jesus: "Oh! I do not want this Precious Blood to be wasted! I will spend my life collecting it for souls!" [36]

### Texts for Meditation

But when Christ appeared as high priest of the good things to come, He entered once for all through the greater and more perfect tabernacle, not made by hands (that is, not of this creation), nor again by virtue of blood of goats and calves, but by virtue of His own blood, into the Holies, having obtained eternal redemption. For if the blood of goats and bulls and the sprinkled ashes of a heifer sanctify the unclean unto the cleansing of the flesh, how much more will the blood of Christ, who through the Holy Spirit offered Himself unblemished unto God, cleanse your conscience from dead works to serve the living God? (Heb. 9:11–14.)

Since then, brethren, we are free to enter the Holies in virtue of the blood of Christ, a new and living way which He inaugurated for us through the veil (that is, flesh), and since we have a high priest over the house of God, let us draw near with a true heart in fullness of faith, having our hearts cleansed from an evil conscience by sprinkling, and the body washed with clean water. (Heb. 10:19–22.)

The Precious Blood belongs in a special manner to men. Much more, therefore, does God invite them to come to its heavenly baths, and receive therein, not only the cleansing of their souls, but the power of a new and amazing life. . . .

[35] Gal. 2:20.          [36] *Novissima Verba*, August 1, 1897.

It is by the Precious Blood of Jesus that the soul becomes ever more and more radiant. It is the secret source of all mystical transformations of the soul into the likeness of its crucified Spouse. . . .

All the new nature of man, who is "renewed in Christ Jesus," comes from this blood, whether it be his love of suffering, his delight in shame, his grace of prayer, his unworldly tastes, his strange humility, his shy concealment, his zeal for souls, his venturous audacity, or his obstinate perseverance. Sinner, saint, and common Christian, all in their own way, require the Precious Blood each moment of their lives; and as the manna in the mouths of the Israelites had the savor which each man wished it to have, so is it with the sweetness, the variety, and the fitness of the graces of the Precious Blood. (Father Faber, *op. cit.,* p. 26.)

We who have been admitted to the holy table, O Lord, have drawn waters with joy from the fountains of the Savior; may His blood, we beseech Thee, be within us as a fountain of water springing up unto eternal life. (Postcommunion, Feast of the Precious Blood.)

# CHAPTER 10 ✍

# *To Christ through Mary*

O Jesus, living in Mary,
Come, and live in Your servants
By Your Spirit of holiness,
By the fullness of Your power,
By the reality of Your virtues,
By the perfection of Your ways,
By the communion of Your Mysteries,
And prevail over all enemy powers.
      Through Your Spirit
For the glory of the Father! Amen.

THIS beautiful invocation, born of the devotion of the Founder of Saint-Sulpice, is well known. But Father Olier's prayer is not only an admirable elevation, it is also a substantial summary of the doctrine of our union with the life-giving humanity of Christ.

In this chapter we shall consider only the first invocation: "O Jesus, living in Mary." These magnificent words summarize an aspect of the dogma of our union with Christ that is too dear to our hearts and too fruitful for the life of our souls to be allowed to remain in the background. Actually, the life of Jesus that we receive through our vital communion with the virtues, states, and mysteries of the God-man, has been communicated in a far superior manner to the Woman who was more closely united to Christ the Savior than any other human being, the Woman who, by this very fact, is the greatest Christian and is totally transformed into the likeness of Jesus. We are speaking, of course, of the Blessed Virgin Mary.

Moreover, the life of Jesus was given to her in super-abundance so that she might communicate it to us through a truly maternal influence—an influence that extends to all the graces received by redeemed men and that makes of her in very truth the New Eve and the spiritual Mother of all the living.

In the plan of divine providence, which treats us with infinite delicacy "and with great favor disposest of us," [1] we are united to Christ and quickened by His life. But we are also closely united and attached to Mary's maternal heart. We receive from her the same graces of holiness and love that spring from the wounded heart of our divine Redeemer. And the more we succeed in yielding ourselves filially to the life-giving action of our Mother, the more completely will we be under the sanctifying influence of Christ's sacred humanity—the humanity that she formed in her virginal womb, nourished from her own sub-stance, possessed with ineffable exclusiveness, to which she continues to be intimately united in glory, and from which she draws the grace and life that she then transmits to all men. We shall develop these fundamental ideas in order to place our Marian devotion on a sound doctrinal basis and to discover an excellent means of uniting our-selves to Jesus and of living by His divine life.

Jesus, living in Mary! Mystery of holiness and love that our poor human minds will never be able to fathom, but to which souls devoted to Mary are instinctively drawn in

[1] Wisd. 12:18

their eagerness to contemplate its beauty, delight in its sweetness, and gather its fruits.

Through the mystery of the Incarnation, Jesus, the Son of God clothed in our humanity, deigned to reside in the womb of the Virgin. "Behold, thou shalt conceive in thy womb . . . and . . . the Holy One to be born shall be called the Son of God." [2] The Son of God made man veiled His majesty and "dwelt among us," [3] as St. John tells us. His dwelling was none other than the immaculate womb of the humble Virgin of Nazareth who had dedicated herself wholly to God. "How shall this happen, since I do not know man?" [4] And since purity brings us near to God [5] and gives us a special affinity with Him, we can surmise the ineffable exchange of love, the union of hearts, and the intimate conversation that took place between the happy Mother and the Infant-God who, from the moment of His conception was fully aware of His life as God and man, and possessed "all the treasures of wisdom and knowledge." [6]

Jesus, living in Mary! Yes, that was truly the case during those nine months of communion between the Blessed Mother and the divine Child she was carrying. But Jesus lived in Mary in another way during His entire earthly life and even afterward, through Mary's close participation in all His mysteries and holy actions. If St. Paul could say of himself that Christ lived in him and if he exhorted the faithful to share the sentiments of Christ ("Have this mind in you which was also in Christ Jesus," [7]), how much more perfectly did the Mother of Jesus share the heart and soul of her beloved Son. To quote the words of St. Pius X:

---

[2] Luke 1:31, 35.       [3] John 1:14.       [4] Luke 1:34.
[5] Cf. Wisd. 6:20: "Incorruption bringeth near to God."
[6] Col. 2:3.       [7] Phil. 2:5.

"With her alone Jesus was associated for thirty years in the closest ties of intimate domestic life. . . . Who more than His Mother was capable of gaining an extensive understanding of the wondrous mysteries of His birth and childhood and above all the mystery of the Incarnation, which is the beginning and the foundation of faith? . . . Hence, no one ever knew Christ so thoroughly as she did, and no one can ever be a more competent guide and teacher for knowing Christ." [8]

It can truly be said that from the moment of the Incarnation Mary's whole life was an uninterrupted communion with the life of her divine Son. It began with the communion of life between Jesus and Mary during the period when the Heart of the Infant-God beat close to the Immaculate Heart of the Virgin Mother. We know from St. Paul that Jesus came into the world to offer Himself to God His Father as a victim of expiation and praise in the name of sinful humanity.[9] How could the Mother not have participated intimately in the reparative function of her Jesus, since she was indissolubly associated to the great work of the Redemption? And from the beginning, the sorrowful heart of Mary sacrificed itself with the Heart of the Holy Victim. She joined with Christ in saying: "Behold, I come to do Thy will, O God!" [10] as soon as He entered the world, just as she had answered the angel: "Behold the handmaid of the Lord; be it done to me according to thy word." [11]

There was a communion of life between Jesus and Mary during His entire earthly existence. There were the long

---

[8] Encyclical *Ad diem illum*, issued February 2, 1904. English translation published by the Marian Library, University of Dayton, Ohio, 1954.

[9] Cf. Heb. 2:17.    [10] Heb. 10:9.    [11] Luke 1:38.

years of intimacy in the solitude of Nazareth when no one except Mary's virginal husband had any notion of the ineffable mystery of the God-man. What an inexhaustible subject for contemplation and what unsounded depths in Mary's heart as she carefully kept the secret of all she saw and heard.[12] Only the silence of a prayerful soul could do fitting honor to these divine realities.

At the marriage feast of Cana something of the intimacy between the Virgin Mary and her Son became manifest. Mary had brought her divine Son and His first disciples to this family feast. Their roles of parent and child were soon to be reversed, and He who had been an obedient Son would show Himself to be the Master, miracle worker, and Messias. It would then be fitting that Mary retire into the background, that the bonds of flesh and blood no longer conceal from the earthy Jews the divine Person of the Savior. But that moment was not yet. Therefore, turning to His Mother, Jesus said: "What wouldst thou have Me do, woman? My hour has not yet come." [13]

These words discouraged Mary not at all, for she knew her Son's heart. She did not even answer Him, but turning to the servants, she said: "Do whatever He tells you." [14] Moved by His Mother, whom He pretended to ignore, Jesus gave orders. He commanded: "Fill the jars with water. . . . Draw out now." [15] We know the rest and we know the secret of Mary's power in inducing Jesus to work miracles and in arousing His disciples' faith in Him.

There was also a communion of life during the painful scenes of Christ's holy passion, during the bloody immolation of the Immaculate Lamb. Mary was close to Jesus when His friends abandoned Him; when the excited

---

[12] *Ibid.*, 2:51.          [13] John 2:4.          [14] *Ibid.*, 2:5.
[15] *Ibid.*, 2:7–8.

crowd insulted Him and demanded His death; when the leaders of Israel blasphemed against Him and sent Him to the gibbet; when the conscience of the Roman Governor who was the guardian of order and justice abdicated before the Jews' clamor and committed the most terrible injustice against this Just Man; and when even the apostles betrayed or denied Him or left Him alone while they took to cowardly flight. Mary, His Mother, united herself to Him throughout the unfolding of the divine sacrifice. "Standing by the cross of Jesus," [16] she generously shared the bitter chalice that the divine Savior willingly drank for the life of our souls. In that solemn moment she became the Mother of all redeemed men by another right, for as the New Eve by the side of the New Adam, she atoned for the sin the first woman committed in conjunction with the sin of the first man.

Jesus' words to His Mother at that moment, "Woman, behold, thy son," [17] took on a deep significance. This "Woman," present at the bloody altar of the divine Redeemer, was the one who had been promised by God to our first parents when He had said to the seducer: "I will put enmities between thee and the woman, and thy seed and her seed; she shall crush thy head." [18] It was she who had been greeted by the angel of the Annunciation: "Blessed art thou among women." [19] And St. John would one day see her in Patmos in a vision of glory: "A woman clothed with the sun, and the moon . . . under her feet, and upon her head a crown of twelve stars." [20] She is the one to whom St. Paul refers as "the woman" of whom Christ was born,[21] pointing her out as the only mother who exclusively

[16] John 19:25.  [17] *Ibid.*, 19:26.  [18] Gen. 3:15.
[19] Luke 1:28.  [20] Apoc. 12:1.
[21] Cf. Gal. 4:4: "God sent His Son, born of a woman."

possesses the fruit of her womb, since she conceived Him virginally whereas all the other children of men are born of the will of man.[22]

Thus Mary reveals herself to us as possessing everywhere and always an intimate communion of life and operation with her beloved Son. We can now understand the words of St. Pius X, cited earlier: "No one ever knew Christ so thoroughly as she did." And the saintly Pope concluded: "No one can ever be a more competent guide and teacher for knowing Christ." [23]

Thus, the Blessed Virgin not only shared the life of her divine Son as His inseparable companion and associate in the work of our salvation, she is also indissolubly united to Him in the transmission of the life of grace which Jesus infuses into us at the present time through the channel of His sacred humanity. How could we possibly have to part company with Mary, the Mother of Jesus, in order to approach her Son, to touch the hem of His sacred garments, to retrace His footsteps through the Gospels, to communicate with His divine mysteries, and to sense power going forth from Him? [24] We need have no fears on that score. Mary was not only united to Christ in the mysteries of His redemptive life; she continues to be associated with Him, by God's most certain will, in the transmission of the grace of these mysteries and in the communication of divine life.

Pope Pius XI called Mary "the minister of grace." [25] For many centuries the devotion of the faithful, with the Church's approval, has saluted her as "Mother of divine

---

[22] Cf. John 1:13.                    [23] Encyclical, *Ad diem illum.*
[24] Cf. Luke 8:46.
[25] Encyclical on reparation to the Sacred Heart, *Miserentissimus,* issued May 8, 1928.

grace." [26] In an even clearer and more magnificent way, St. Pius X calls her "the chief minister of the graces to be dispensed." [27]

Was it not through Mary's voice that Jesus communicated the first sanctifying grace of His sacred humanity? When Elizabeth received the Blessed Virgin's visit, the Precursor leaped for joy in his mother's womb, sensing the hidden presence of the Word Incarnate. The interior light that flooded the unborn John was an infusion of grace granted by Jesus through the living sacrament of His Mother.

But we must go back even further to find the root of this power over grace that the Church and the saints have attributed to the Blessed Virgin. It is to be found in the very mystery of the Incarnation, at that solemn moment which lies at the center of all history, when the Son of God was conceived by the operation of the Holy Ghost in the womb of the Blessed Virgin, uniting His divinity to a tiny parcel of mortal humanity. It was then that Mary became both the Mother of God and the Mother of men: the Mother of God according to the flesh, and the Mother of men according to the spirit; the Mother of Jesus according to nature and the Mother of Jesus' brothers according to grace. When Mary conceived Christ according to His own human nature she was, as it were, impregnated with the power of His divinity. In that instant all men became her children, and it was given to her to transmit supernatural life to men, that life of which her Son was at once the exemplar and the source.

This is the beautiful doctrine of St. Louis-Marie de Montfort, which St. Pius X incorporated as his own in the Encyclical *Ad diem illum*. To quote the fiery French apostle: "If Jesus Christ, the Head of men, is born in her,

[26] Litany of the Blessed Virgin.     [27] Encyclical *Ad diem illum*.

then the predestined, who are members of that Head, ought also to be born in her by a necessary consequence. One and the same mother does not bring forth into the world the head without the members or the members without the head; . . . and if a member of the Mystical Body of Jesus Christ—that is to say, one of the predestined —were born of any other mother than Mary, who has produced the Head, he would not be one of the predestined, nor a member of Jesus Christ, but simply a monster in the order of grace." [28]

With even greater authority, St. Pius X teaches: "Thus in one and the same bosom of the most chaste Mother, Christ took to Himself flesh and joined to Himself the spiritual body formed by those who were to believe in Him. And so in carrying the Savior within her, Mary may be said to have carried at the same time all those whose life was contained in the life of the Savior. All of us, then, who are united with Christ and are, in the words of the Apostle, 'members of His body, made from His flesh and from His bones' (Eph. 5:30), have really come forth from the womb of Mary as a body united with its head. Hence, in a spiritual and mystical sense, we are all Mary's children, and she is the Mother of all of us." [29]

It follows that the maternal action of Mary upon our souls is inseparable from the life-giving influence of Jesus and every grace that comes to us from the sacred humanity of our divine Savior passes through the hands of His most holy Mother. In the words of Pope Leo XIII: "Since she served as intermediary in the work of Redemption, she likewise exercises her mediatory action in the com-

---

[28] *Treatise on the True Devotion to the Blessed Virgin Mary,* (Ottawa: Librairie Mariale, 1941), Fourth Edition, pp. 23–24.
[29] Encyclical *Ad diem illum.*

munication of the grace that flows from this mystery through the centuries, and to this end she has been endowed with an almost unlimited power." [30]

That is why the Holy Ghost secretly awakens an attraction for Mary in every soul that desires to be intimately united to Jesus and share in His divine life. And just as the Father has given us the Spirit of His Son to cry out to Him: "Abba, Father!" [31] so it can be said without exaggeration that every child of God receives on his baptismal day the same divine Spirit to cry out to Mary: "Mother!" Father Olier went so far as to say: "God the Father attaches all His children to this adorable womb, to this most lovable womb [of Mary], and the Church deems herself infinitely fortunate each day because the blood and substance of Jesus Christ is changed for her into milk within the breast of the Blessed Virgin." [32] With this bold and expressive symbolism, so well suited to Mary's maternal role with regard to Jesus and His Church, this pious author has given an exact rendition of the doctrine of Mary's mediation of grace and her sanctifying influence upon all the members of the Mystical Body, in dependence upon the vital influence of Jesus.

The influence of Mary on our sanctification is closely related to the doctrine of the sanctifying mysteries of our Lord, which we have presented earlier.[33] In that connection we said that a precious means of appropriating the riches contained in the sacred humanity of our divine Savior is to unite ourselves with one or another of His mysteries, to communicate through lively faith, hope, and love in one of the virtues, states, activities, or attitudes of

[30] Encyclical *Adjutricem populi*, September 5, 1893.
[31] Gal. 4:6; Rom. 8:15.                [32] Letter 119, Migne edition.
[33] Cf. chapter III.

the God-man. For all these mysteries are holy and sanctifying in the measure that we have recourse to them through faith. "Someone touched Me; for I perceived that power had gone forth from me." [34]

And yet of all these mysteries of the Savior there is one, as St. Pius X tells us, that is fundamental: the mystery of His incarnation in the womb of Mary, the mystery of His vital dependence upon His Mother. This mystery is therefore as divine, salutary, holy and sanctifying as the others, if not more so.

This is the theological explanation and the justification of the attitude of so many souls who have sought to find Jesus by filial submission to Mary, by union with Mary, and even by losing themselves ineffably in Mary—in the virginal womb that once held Jesus and continues to bear and to form the brothers of Jesus. The Holy Ghost must orientate souls in this direction, but it is also important to show the doctrinal relationship between an intense Marian life and the general dogma of the Incarnation and the sanctification of souls through the humanity of the Word made flesh.

This, too, is the doctrine of St. Louis-Marie de Montfort: "It is certain that Jesus Christ is, for each man in particular who possesses Him, as truly the fruit of the womb of Mary as He is for the whole world in general. . . . We can apply to her [Mary] more than St. Paul applied to himself the words: 'I am in labor again with all the children of God, until Jesus Christ my Son be formed in them in the fullness of His age.'" [35]

Just as Mary became fruitful in Nazareth through the action of the Holy Ghost, so also through this same divine Spirit the Blessed Virgin acts within our souls. "God the

[34] Luke 8:46.                    [35] *True Devotion,* pp. 24–25.

Holy Ghost . . . is become fruitful by Mary, whom He has espoused." [36] So true is this that a sure means of attracting the sanctifying Spirit to dwell within us is to unite ourselves intimately to Mary and to introduce her into our souls. As St. Louis-Marie says: "When the Holy Ghost . . . has found Mary in a soul, He flies there. He enters there in His fullness; He communicates Himself to that soul abundantly and to the full extent to which it makes room for His Spouse." [37] This is the mystery of our life in Christ through Mary. Jesus, by reason of His humanity, is indeed the universal Mediator; but Mary is a subordinate Mediatrix in the entire work of salvation.

How does the divine Mother exercise her power over grace in the work of our sanctification? How does she give the life of Christ to her children? How is her maternal action joined to the vital influence of the Word Incarnate? We do not need an exhaustive explanation of all these things in order to sustain the fervor of our filial piety toward Mary. Such an analysis can only be part of the general theology of the supernatural causality of grace through the Word Incarnate and through the sacraments.[38] What has been said to establish the *fact* of Mary's influence provides devout souls with a solid foundation for their devotion to Mary. As to the *how* of our Mother's intervention in our divine life, let us say briefly that it is realized in two ways which actually merge into a single action: 1) the Blessed Virgin intercedes for us; 2) the Blessed Virgin acts upon us. She prays and she has an operative influence; she acts before God and she acts upon

[36] *Ibid.,* p. 15.          [37] *Ibid.,* p. 27.
[38] A full treatment of this subject will be found in Marie-Vincent Bernadot, O.P., *Our Lady in Our Life,* translated by Mary Ryan (Westminster, Md.: The Newman Press, 1950), pp. 36 ff. and pp. 53–61.

us. But her intervention before God is identical with her action upon our souls, because it is Mary's very prayer, filled with divine power, that acts efficaciously upon us and communicates to us the supernatural life of grace.

The Blessed Virgin Mary intercedes for us. We have seen an instance of it in the marriage feast of Cana, which was the prelude to so many of Mary's interventions in the life of the Church and in the life of souls. It is the universal belief of the faithful and the common teaching of the Doctors and the saints that Mary intercedes for us. Even in the catacombs, the early Christians translated this faith by representing the divine Mother as a Virgin in prayer. Even today our liturgy calls her our "Advocate," [39] and constantly calls upon her powerful and glorious intercession.

St. Pius X sums up this universal teaching as follows: "The Virgin from heaven above keeps watch over us and strives with unceasing prayer to complete the number of the elect." [40] By unceasing prayer! Did not the Blessed Virgin appear at La Salette on September 19, 1846, to remind us tearfully: "If my people will not submit, I shall be forced to let go of my Son's arm. I am obliged to pray unceasingly. You would never be able to repay me for all the trouble I have taken for you!"

It should give us great confidence to know that our Mother is so full of solicitude for us, her children, and so assiduous, too, in interceding with her Son for those who do not appreciate her maternal love. But the Blessed Virgin does more than pray. She also acts upon us, cultivates our souls, and, dependent upon Jesus, brings forth the life of grace within us. As Pope Pius XI has said, she is "the minister of grace." The writers we have cited have com-

[39] The *Salve Regina*.           [40] Encyclical *Ad diem illum*.

pared Mary's maternal influence to the influence she had on Jesus when He dwelt within her virginal womb, and St. Pius X went so far as to declare that the Blessed Virgin is the neck through which the Head exercises His power and virtue on His Mystical Body.[41]

Speaking of Mary's influence on the human race since her glorious Assumption, Father de Condren says that she tends to "annihilate man and bring forth God in man." He adds: "This is the principal action of the Holy Mother of God upon us, and the one that we must desire above all else that she have upon us." [42]

This is what St. Louis-Marie de Montfort means when he speaks of Mary's fruitfulness through the Holy Ghost: "We may evidently conclude, then, from what I have said, first of all, that Mary has received from God a great domination over the souls of the elect; for she cannot make her residence in them as God the Father ordered her to do; and, as their mother, form, nourish and bring them forth to eternal life; and have them as her inheritance and portion; and form them in Jesus Christ and Jesus Christ in them; and strike the roots of her virtues in their hearts and be the inseparable companion of the Holy Ghost in all His works of grace—she cannot, I say, do all these things unless she has a right and a domination over their souls by a singular grace of the Most High who, having given her power over His only and natural Son, has given it also to her over His adopted children, not only as to their bodies, which would be but a small matter, but also as to their souls." [43]

---

[41] Encyclical *Ad diem illum.*

[42] Lettres du Père Charles de Condren (Paris: Éditions du Cerf, 1943).

[43] *True Devotion,* pp. 27–28.

Mary is a Mother, and a mother communicates life to the fruit of her womb through her whole being. But how are we to conceive of Mary's maternal action? How does this action fit in with her prayer? It is the same problem as in the case of Christ, and the solution is identical. In all things Mary is a mediatrix through her prayer and her sanctifying influence. Jesus continues to pray in heaven, the Apostle teaches us. As man, He prays for us continually: "He lives always to make intercession for [us]." [44] But St. Thomas tells us that Christ's prayer is clothed with power. His human will, subject to the all-powerful will of God, is at once suppliant and operative. The prayer of Jesus, like all the other actions of His sacred humanity, is filled with the divine power of the Word. Christ's prayer, which is the expression of His human will, is a petition to God and a command to men. Moreover, His commands are efficacious, and effect what they express. We have many examples of this in the Gospels. When the leper begged to be cured, Jesus said: "I will; be thou made clean," [45] and the disease obeyed His voice. Indeed, every creature feels the power of His commands.

Now, it is in the same line of thought that we must seek to understand Mary's prayer and sanctifying action. Mary is united to her divine Son always and everywhere, and she shares all His prerogatives as fully as any creature can. She has received a communication of Jesus' universal power, and everything that is subject to Christ also obeys Mary. St. Louis-Marie tells us: "The authority which God has been well pleased to give her is so great that it seems as if she had the same power as God and as if her prayers and petitions are so powerful with God that they always

[44] Heb. 7:25.                    [45] Matt. 8:3.

pass for commandments with His Majesty." [46] "The will of the Most High, who exalts the humble Mary whom He has made the sovereign of heaven and earth, general of His armies, treasurer of His treasures, dispenser of His graces, worker of His greatest marvels." [47]

Mary's will, always submissive to the royal authority of her Son, faithfully accepts all His sanctifying desires. She enters into all the plans of Christ the Savior, not only as a humble servant but as an associate in the work of redemption. In the words of Pope Leo XIII, she is "the minister of the sacrament of man's redemption." [48] Mary's active role at her Son's side, dependent upon His redemptive mission, gives her will the efficacy and sanctifying power that belong properly to the will of Christ Himself. That is how Mary becomes in very truth "the worker of God's greatest marvels," to use St. Louis-Marie de Montfort's words. She acts upon her children, in union with Jesus, to bring them forth to grace. She acts upon every creature to make it serve God's great plans for the world. "That universal action [of Mary's] over creation, the very thought of which makes us dizzy," says Father Bernadot, "does not exceed the unique power of the Mother of God. Her immense sway is exercised every moment by perfect acts, diverse and multiple, strong and tender, reaching out to each soul and to the whole Christ whom she envelopes in love. Her hidden action, so gentle and delicate, is ever imperceptibly operative on the created universe. One of the realities that the Church was quickest to feel was the guidance of Our Lady's invisible action and her all-pervading maternal influence. She is present to

[46] *True Devotion*, p. 20.    [47] *Ibid.*, p. 21.
[48] Encyclical *Adjutricem populi*, September 5, 1893.

every soul, with a spiritual presence that is a beautiful reality." [49]

Fortunate is the soul that knows how to dispose itself to receive the grace of Mary's maternal, efficacious, and sanctifying presence, or that Mary herself predisposes to receive it! The whole orientation of this grace is to form Jesus within us, Jesus her firstborn [50] and only Son. "Until Christ is formed in you!" [51] This Marian doctrine justifies the richest, most-inclusive, and total devotion to Mary, as well as the utmost in holy audacity on the part of her children. The conclusion to which it leads is this: our filial union with Mary is simply one aspect, eminent and privileged, of life-giving union with the humanity of Christ, her divine Son. There are countless ways of expressing this life of union with Mary, but devotion to the Holy Rosary is one which seems particularly fruitful and a most excellent means of uniting us habitually with Jesus through Mary.

### Texts for Meditation

I have trodden under my feet the hearts of all the high and low: and in all these I sought rest, . . .

Then the Creator of all things commanded, and said to me: and He that made me, rested in my tabernacle. And He said to me: Let they dwelling be in Jacob, and thy inheritance in Israel, and take root in My elect. . . .

And so was I established in Sion, and in the holy city likewise I rested, and my power *was* in Jerusalem. And I took root in an honorable people, and in the portion of my God His inheritance, . . .

Come over to me, all ye that desire me, and be filled with my

[49] M.-V. Bernadot, O.P., *Our Lady in Our Life,* pp. 33-34.
[50] Cf. Luke 2:7.                    [51] Gal. 4:19.

fruits. For my spirit is sweet above honey, and my inheritance above honey and the honeycomb.

They that eat me, shall yet hunger: and they that drink me, shall yet thirst.

He that harkeneth to me, shall not be confounded: and they that work by me, shall not sin. (Ecclus. 24:11–30.)

Now therefore, ye children, hear me: Blessed are they that keep my ways. Hear instruction and be wise, and refuse it not.

Blessed is the man that heareth me, and that watcheth daily at my gates, and waiteth at the posts of my doors. He that shall find me, shall find life, and shall have salvation from the Lord. (Prov. 8:32–35.)

The conduct which the Three Persons of the Most Holy Trinity have deigned to pursue in the Incarnation and the first coming of Jesus Christ, They still pursue daily, in an invisible manner, throughout the whole Church; and They will still pursue it even to the consummation of ages in the last coming of Jesus Christ.

God the Father wishes to have children by Mary till the consumation of the world; and He speaks to her these words: "Dwell in Jacob"; that is to say: Make your dwelling and residence in My predestined children, prefigured by Jacob, and not in the reprobate children of the devil, prefigured by Esau.

Just as in the natural and corporal generation of children there are a father and a mother, so in the supernatural and spiritual generation there are a Father, who is God, and a Mother, who is Mary. All the true children of God, the predestinate, have God for their Father and Mary for their Mother. He who has not Mary for his Mother has not God for his Father. . . .

God the Son wishes to form Himself and, so to speak, to incarnate Himself in His members every day, by His dear Mother, and He says to her: "Take Israel for your inheritance."

It is as if He had said: God the Father has given Me for an inheritance all the nations of the earth, all the men good and bad, predestinate and reprobate. Those I will lead with a rod of gold, and these with a rod of iron. . . . But as for you, My dear Mother, you shall have for your heritage and possession only the predestinate, prefigured by Israel; and as their Mother, you shall bring them forth and take care of them; and as their sovereign, you shall conduct them, govern them, and defend them.

Jesus being at present as much as ever the fruit of Mary—as heaven and earth repeat thousands and thousands of times a day, "and blessed is the fruit of thy womb, Jesus"—it is certain that Jesus Christ is, for each man in particular who possesses Him, as truly the fruit of the womb of Mary as He is for the whole world in general. . . .

God the Holy Ghost wishes to form elect for Himself in her and by her, and He says to her: "Strike the roots," My well Beloved and My Spouse, "of all your virtues in My elect," in order that they may grow from virtue to virtue and from grace to grace. . . .

When Mary has struck her roots in a soul, she produces there marvels of grace, which she alone can produce, because she alone is the fruitful Virgin who never has had, and never will have, her equal, in purity and in fruitfulness.

When the Holy Ghost, her Spouse, has found Mary in a soul, He flies there. He enters there in His fullness; He communicates Himself to that soul abundantly, and to the full extent to which it makes room for His Spouse. (St. Louis-Marie de Montfort, *True Devotion,* nos. 22–36.)

O Mary, Mother of God and my tender Mother, cover me with the fleece of the Lamb who was formed from your substance. Through you, may He who is the supreme love receive me, feed me, possess me, govern me, and make me perfect!

Hail, O Mary, Queen of mercy, through whom the remedy of life has come to us; Virgin and Mother of the divine offspring, you through whom He who is the eternal light has come to us, He who pours forth His perfumes upon Israel.

In your Son you became the true Mother of all men, whose brother this only Son of your womb deigned to become. For His love, receive me in my unworthiness into your mother's arms.

Help my faith, preserve it, and enlighten it; be a principle of renewal and fidelity within me, O my most loving and only Mother! Surround me with your most merciful care during this life, and receive me at the hour of my death to your maternal breast. Amen. (St. Gertrude.)

# CHAPTER 11 &

# *The Rosary*

"HE that shall find me, shall find life." [1] The Church places these words on Mary's lips in the liturgy. We have given a brief outline of the sublime mystery of Mary, which complements the mystery of Jesus. The Mother of Jesus, as we have seen, is intimately united with Christ, her divine Son, in the work of grace. Now we must introduce into our own lives the close bond that God Himself has established between the Blessed Virgin and her Son, in order not to separate what God has united.

Grace attracts souls to Mary in many different ways. There is such admirable variety in the Marian devotion of devout souls and in the lives of the saints that the words of Wisdom are applicable to each one of them: "There was not found the like to him in glory." [2] Marian devotion is more dominant in some than in others. There are those whose love for the Blessed Virgin shines forth in certain periods of their life, afterwards being overshadowed, only to reappear with renewed brilliance at the end. In the case of others, Marian devotion fills their whole life to such an intense degree that everything they do is through Mary and under her maternal influence. It is a great joy to compare the lives of the saints in this connection, but we must be careful not to take a superficial view. There

[1] Prov. 8:35.      [2] Ecclus. 44:20.

are saints—as Father Genevois showed in the case of St. Catherine of Siena [3]—who seemed completely absorbed by the mystery of Christ and His Church, but whose spirituality, when examined closely, shows itself to be penetrated with a very deep Marian piety.

Devotion to Mary also varies in orientation. Some souls go directly to Mary and through her maternal mediation soon reach the Heart of Christ, her beloved Son. Others go to Jesus, the one Mediator, and by force of circumstances find themselves in Mary's sweet company. While the classical formula, *Ad Jesum per Mariam,* is ontologically exact in terms of speculative theology, it does not adequately translate the actual process by which all souls in the practice of the interior life attain to the relationships of faith and love with Jesus and His divine Mother.

For example, in the spirituality of that incomparable master Dom Marmion, Marian devotion finds comparatively sober expression, whereas Mary assumes an extraordinary place in the life of his beloved disciple, Dom Pius de Hemptinne. On June 23, 1901, Dom Pius wrote to his spiritual father: "I can no longer hide from you an important favor that Jesus granted me scarcely a month ago. He united my heart to the heart of our good Mother Mary. I can live with her as well as with Jesus without any rosary, without anything except love. It is impossible to think of Jesus Christ without thinking of Mary. We unite ourselves to Jesus in order to love Mary, and we seek refuge in the heart of Mary to abandon ourselves to Jesus with the almost infinite fullness of love that she had for Him." [4]

[3] Cf. "Douce Marie" in *La Vie Spirituelle,* May, 1947.
[4] Cf. *Un disciple de Dom Marmion,* by Dom Thibaut. (This letter is not included in the English translation.)

Such union with Mary quickly produced its normal fruit:
life with Jesus. Speaking to his heavenly Mother, Dom de
Hemptinne said: "You were the first to teach me to walk
in the path of intimate union with your divine Son. This
year I am consecrated to Jesus hidden in your womb.
Therefore I want to live with you, for I feel only one
need: to belong to Jesus in order to belong to the Father." [5]

The same constant desire to find Jesus by His Mother's
side is revealed in the Marian life of Father Jacquier, who
was powerfully drawn toward the Immaculate Heart of
Mary. In 1935 he wrote: "My only concern will be to
strive to live *in sinu Mariae*. The Heart of Mary will be
my center. I want to lose myself in it and forget everything.
That is the only path for finding Jesus and the Blessed
Trinity." [6]

Thus, there are different paths to follow. The forms
of the Marian cult vary from one soul to another, according
to the movements of grace and the inspirations of the Holy
Ghost, but the end in view is always life in Christ. As
St. Louis-Marie de Montfort says: "The strongest inclination of Mary is to unite us to Jesus Christ, her Son; and
the strongest inclination of the Son is that we should come
to Him through His holy Mother." [7] He completes his
thought by addressing himself directly to our Lord: "Thou,
Lord, art always with Mary, and Mary is always with Thee,
and she cannot be without Thee, else she would cease to
be what she is. She is so transformed into Thee by grace
that she lives no more, and she is as though she were not.

[5] *Ibid.*
[6] *Vie et Doctrine Mariale du P. Jacquier,* by Father Doury (Paris,
1946).
[7] *True Devotion,* p. 63.

It is Thou only, my Jesus, who livest and reignest in her." [8]

In other words, to find Mary is to find the life that is in Christ.

Among the many different forms of Marian devotion, there is one which seems to embrace them all in a superlative degree, for it realizes more perfectly than any other the life of union with Jesus and His mysteries. This devotion is the Holy Rosary. When the Rosary is rightly understood, recited with recollected attention to the admirable prayers that compose it, and vivified by meditation upon Christ's mysteries and those of His Holy Mother, it offers unsuspected riches of life and treasures of grace to receptive souls.

St. Louis-Marie sounded the following warning: "Beware, please beware of looking upon this practice as trifling and of little consequence, as do the vulgar and certain conceited scholars. It is really great, sublime, and divine." [9] Today we no longer have to fight the prejudices that St. Louis-Marie de Montfort encountered in his time. The encyclicals of Pope Leo XIII on the Rosary have placed this devotion in a privileged position among religious practices. Moreover, the prescription of the Code of Canon Law which requires clerics to introduce the Rosary in their daily spiritual regime, on an equal footing with mental prayer and visits to the Blessed Sacrament,[10] should be of great significance to everyone. In addition, Mary herself has extended many pressing invitations to her

[8] *Ibid.*, p. 51.
[9] *The Secret of the Rosary* (Montfort Fathers Publications), Introduction.
[10] Canon 125, 2.

children through the ages, urging them to recite the Rosary. As St. Louis-Marie has pointed out: "It was necessary for the Blessed Virgin to appear several times to great and enlightened saints to show them the merit of [the Rosary]. She did so to St. Dominic, St. John Capistrano, and Blessed Alan de la Roche. They have composed entire treatises on the wonders and efficacy of that prayer for converting souls." [11] What would St. Louis-Marie say today, after the apparitions at Lourdes and the message of our Lady of the Rosary at Fátima?

Evidently, devotion to the Holy Rosary needs no further recommendation. However, we do need a better understanding of its nature; we also need to vivify our recitation of it, so that it may become what Our Lady wants it to be: a means of union with our Lord.

Meditation upon the mysteries is the soul of the Holy Rosary and gives it sanctifying power. It is through contemplation of the life of Jesus and Mary that the Rosary becomes not only a beneficial pious practice like any other prayer, but a way of perfection, a ladder to holiness, a means of transforming souls through communion with the dispositions of Christ and His holy Mother.

St. Paul told the Christians: "Have this mind in you which was also in Christ Jesus." [12] But is there any better way of penetrating into Christ's mind than to meditate upon the mysteries of the Rosary? By the prolonged contact with Jesus and Mary which the Rosary makes possible, the soul gradually learns to "comprehend . . . what is the breadth and length and height and depth" [13] of the mystery of Christ, "Christ's love which surpasses knowledge," [14] and "the unfathomable riches" [15] of His sacred

---

[11] *True Devotion*, p. 217.        [12] Phil. 2:5.
[13] Eph. 3:18.        [14] *Ibid.*, 3:19.        [15] *Ibid.*, 3:8.

soul. The Rosary unfolds the whole economy of God's mysteries in the work of salvation and sanctification.

The mysteries of the Holy Rosary and the prayers that accompany them provide the Christian soul with a sublime view of all the divine realities to enlighten faith and nourish love. As Bishop Gay has pointed out: "All the great and necessary objects of our faith are really contained in the *Hail Mary* and the *Our Father* for anyone who is capable of understanding: the unity and nature of God and the Trinity of Persons; His perfections and providence; the Incarnation of the Word and the redemption of the human race by the Word Incarnate; the existence, nature, and ministry of the good angels and the state and the activities of the bad angels; the Immaculate Conception, perpetual virginity, and divine maternity of Mary; the immortality of our souls and the condition to which sin has reduced us; our justification by grace, our adoption as children of God, our heavenly destiny, our hopes with their immutable foundation, our inevitable struggles and the secret of victory, and the need of God's help in order to persevere in the right; our duties to God, to Christ, to Mary, to the saints, to our neighbor, and finally to ourselves. . . . And if we add to these prayers the succession of mysteries upon which we meditate while praying vocally—and this meditation is of the very essence of the Rosary—the Rosary would seem to contain the whole of Christianity." [16]

In the crown of roses into which the holy mysteries are interwoven, the truths of faith are filled with unction and adorned with supernatural poetry. In the words of the author just cited: "The Rosary is the [Apostles'] creed in flowers, the great and solid creed of the Word, trans-

[16] *Les Mystères du saint Rosaire* (Paris, 1887).

formed by the Holy Ghost into a living perfume that is breathed forth by our souls and which rejoices the heart of God, passing through Mary's heart and through our own." [17]

Let no one think that meditation upon the mysteries of the Rosary is beyond the ordinary capacity of even the simplest souls. If the faithful are shown how to say the Rosary in this way, they can derive from it the fruits of grace contained in each of these mysteries. Indeed, the soul of every baptized Christian possesses this gift of faith which is always ready to be put to use and to grow, providing it is shown its divine object. The crowds to whom St. Louis-Marie de Montfort communicated his love of the Rosary were ordinary Christians who had been enlightened and encouraged to practice this devotion through an apostle's zeal. The same is true of the thousands of soldiers whom Father Bellanger of Arras taught to share his passion for the Rosary. So well did these men understand and love the devotion that they spent their whole nights on watch saying their beads, without feeling the slightest boredom. [18]

---

[17] *Ibid.*

[18] Father Bellanger formed a military group in Arras under the name of *Notre-Dame du Bon Conseil.* Speaking of these soldiers, he said: "Our young men recite the rosary everywhere. For almost eighteen months several of them have been going every evening to Notre-Dame des Ardents to recite their rosary at Mary's feet. . . . I know two of them who for several months mounted their hour of guard in honor of the Blessed Virgin from nine to ten every evening. But almost all of them converse with her, so to speak, during their long hours on guard during the day or night, their gun in one hand and their rosary in the other. As they sometime tell me, it makes the hours shorter and their knapsack lighter."

Father Bellanger had his method of the Rosary, made up of prayer and affectionate meditation upon the mysteries, and he knew how to communicate his method to others. "Let us not give the common

To meditate upon the mysteries of the Rosary, the faithful do not need to know how to carry on long reflections. All they have to do is to *look* at Jesus and Mary during the whole recitation of the Rosary: to look at Jesus conceived by Mary, carried by Mary, offered by Mary in the Temple; to look at Jesus praying and undergoing His agony in the Garden, Jesus made prisoner, scourged, crowned with thorns, bearing the weight of the Cross, Jesus dying for us on the gibbet and washing us in His blood; to look at Jesus in the glory of His resurrection, in the triumph of His ascension, quickening the Church by His Spirit, and crowning His Mother in heaven.

At other times, the eye of the soul will focus more upon Mary, the Mother of Jesus: Mary united to Jesus, Mary sharing the life of Jesus, Mary the perfect Christian, totally conformed to Christ in His mysteries, acting for Him and with Him, suffering like Him and because of Him, glorified with Him and in Him. And while the *Ave's* are recited, the soul will keep its interior gaze fixed on Jesus and Mary. It will bless Mary, full of grace, full of the grace the Holy Ghost poured into her at the Annunciation, full of the grace which she shared with Elizabeth and John the Baptist at her Visitation, and growing continually in grace in the mysteries of Christmas, the Presentation, the Finding in the Temple, and the long, silent life in Nazareth. And so on for the other mysteries.

---

people a theory drawn solely from books," he said. "Let us allow the devotion of the Holy Rosary to possess us, and to this end let us eat a good meal of the Rosary every day. When this devotion has entered our blood, when we have understood by practical experience that each prayer, each mystery is a mine, an ocean of grace and delight, an earthly paradise, we shall have only one desire: to preach the Holy Rosary and to throw out this lifeline to all souls."

The soul will ponder now one and now another of the phrases in the *Our Father* and in the *Hail Mary*. It will repeat the angel's words to Mary: "The Lord is with thee!" With thee, by thy divine maternity in the Annunciation; with thee in the living tabernacle of thy virginal womb, when thou didst bear thy Son to Zachary's house; with thee on thy breast, when thou didst take Jesus to Jerusalem, and later when thou didst find Him in the Temple; with thee near the Cross, with thee in glory!

"Blessed art thou among women": blessed in the honor of thy holy and virginal Maternity, in all the mysteries of thy boundless joy; blessed in the untold sorrows of thy Compassion, from the Garden to Calvary; blessed in the shining forth of thy glory, united to that of thy beloved Son.

"Blessed is the fruit of thy womb," the sweet Savior Jesus! Blessed is He in the merciful condescension of His incarnation; blessed in the sanctifying mysteries of His childhood and His most holy life; blessed in His agony in the Garden, His scourging and crowning with thorns, in the burning thirst He suffered on the Cross; blessed in His testament of love by which He bequeathed His Mother to us! Yes, blessed is the divine Savior, who died and rose again for us to bury us with Him in baptism and bring us forth again to a new life!

The soul need not formulate all these thoughts explicitly in its prayer, but simply cast a look of faith on Jesus and upon Mary united to Jesus. Through this look of faith and love, the divine mystery will enter into the soul and mark it more and more in the likeness of Christ the Redeemer. In this way, the recitation of the Rosary will become one of the most fruitful and sanctifying exercises of the Christian life. Through the Rosary the faithful will once again learn who Christ is and who they are. They will rediscover themselves as members of Christ and as the mystical extension of the Word Incarnate.

To facilitate meditation on the mysteries of the Rosary, enough time should be allowed before each decade for a comprehensive and prolonged look at the whole economy of the mystery in question. When the Rosary is recited privately, what is to prevent the soul from taking its time, following its inward inclinations, saying the *Our Father* and the *Hail Mary* in leisurely fashion, and savoring each word, one at a time, while keeping its gaze fixed lovingly on Jesus and Mary?

During the time for mental prayer, for example, we might well take a half-hour to say five decades of the Rosary. This can easily become the path to a very intimate and profound union with Christ and His divine Mother. What if we sometimes let our rosary fall from our fingers when our soul has risen up to God by the ladder of the mysteries? [19] The Rosary can thus become a school of training in mental prayer, and this prayer, so simple in appearance, can lead the soul to the secret of mystical contemplation. Is this not the goal of our union with the mysteries of our Redemption, which Jesus and Mary accomplished to open heaven's treasures to us?

This is the path that led St. Louis-Marie de Montfort, the apostle of the Rosary, to the highest levels of contemplation. Already in his seminary days, when on a pilgrimage to Chartres with a friend, he spent most of his time at Mary's feet in rapturous silence. Later on, during

---

[19] It is of the utmost importance that the soul's freedom be safeguarded and that it be not bound to any rigid method of prayer. Sometimes the Holy Spirit invites the soul to set aside its ordinary ways in order to follow His inspiration. "The Spirit breathes where He will."

his apostolic missions, he would make retreats two or
three times a year, spending entire days in the refreshment of prolonged mental prayer.

In his *Treatise on the True Devotion to the Blessed
Virgin* he often speaks of mental prayer and of union with
God, to which he means to lead souls by the delightful
path of Marian devotion. In his own words: "Spiritual
persons, therefore, must not fall into the false belief that
Mary can be a hindrance to them in attaining divine
union; for is it possible that she who has found grace before
God for the whole world in general and for each one in
particular, should be a hindrance to a soul in finding the
great grace of union with Him? Can it be possible that
she who has been full and superabounding with graces,
so united and transformed into God that it has been a
kind of necessity that He should be incarnate in her,
should be a stumbling-block in the way of a soul's perfect
union with God?" [20] He then concludes: "Be persuaded,
then, that the more you look at Mary in your prayers,
contemplations, actions, and sufferings, if not with a distinct and definite view, at least with a general and imper-
ceptible one, the more perfectly will you find Jesus Christ,
who is always with Mary, great, powerful, operative and
incomprehensible." [21]

Referring more specifically to the Holy Rosary, he ad-
vises interior souls: "Devout souls enlightened by the Holy
Ghost, you will not be offended if I give you a little mystical rose bush from heaven, to plant in the garden of your
soul. It will not harm the fragrant flowers of your contemplations. . . . Cultivate and water it by faithfully re-
citing it every day and by doing good works, and you will
see that this seed which now seems so small will become a

[20] *True Devotion*, p. 142.          [21] *Ibid.*, p. 143.

great tree where the birds of the sky, that is, the souls that have been predestined and raised to contemplation, will make their nests and their dwellings." [22]

There is nothing surprising in this, since the perfection of the interior life consists in union with Jesus, and meditation upon the mysteries of the Rosary is a choice means of attaining to this union. The *Hail Mary* is itself an abyss of supernatural marvels which brings us back to the great mystery of the Incarnation wherein Jesus accomplished the work of sanctification through Mary. Thus the Rosary, as St. Louis-Marie says, is "that prayer well said which makes the word of God germinate in our souls and bring forth Jesus Christ, the Fruit of Life." [23]

Everything that has been said so far about the Rosary is applicable to the *Hail Mary* in particular. The *Hail Mary* is a world of wonders which the saints never tire of praising and which interior souls never weary of repeating with ever-renewed joy and ever greater fruits of grace. St. Louis-Marie has composed a veritable garland of titles glorifying the Angelical Salutation, and Father Bellanger, his worthy imitator, was constantly praising the beauty and fruitfulness of this prayer.

To quote St. Louis-Marie again: "The *Hail Mary* well said—that is, with attention, devotion and modesty—is, according to the saints, the enemy of the devil which puts him to flight, and the hammer which crushes him. It is the sanctification of the soul, the joy of the angels, the melody of the predestinate, the canticle of the New Testament, the pleasure of Mary, and the glory of the most Holy Trinity. The *Hail Mary* is the heavenly dew which fertilizes the soul. It is the chaste and loving kiss which

[22] *The Admirable Secret of the Most Holy Rosary.*
[23] *True Devotion,* p. 218.

we give to Mary. It is a vermilion rose which we present to her; a precious pearl we offer her." [24]

Actually the *Hail Mary* contains the substance of all the mysteries of the Rosary. By bringing us back to the great fact of the Incarnation, it unites us to Jesus and Mary in the enduring mystery of the Son of God made man, of Christ united to His Mother, enriching her with His graces, saving the world in union with her, sanctifying men through her, and remaining, both in His birth and in His spiritual growth in souls the blessed fruit of her womb.

The *Hail Mary* thus becomes a privileged means of union with Christ and of spiritual communion with His life-giving humanity, providing we know how to reach beyond the words to the divine realities that they express. Then we learn to bow with the archangel with deepest respect before the living tabernacle of God which Mary is, so simple in her grandeur and so great in her humility. Then we salute in the name of all creatures the one who is full of grace, the Mother of God, the Queen of the world. Then we recognize in her, as did an ancient author: "the path of life which the King of heaven blazed when He came to us, and by which we return to Him." [25]

The path of life! Mary is certain to become the path of life for the soul that meditates on the *Hail Mary* or on the Rosary in its every detail. The thoughts and wishes of such a person will be those of Christ and His divine Mother. His actions and endeavors will be modeled upon the Exemplar he constantly contemplates through the holy mysteries. This is what Bishop Gay meant when he called the Rosary "the itinerary of the soul toward God."

[24] *True Devotion,* p. 220.
[25] Adam de Perseigne, Migne, P.L. 211, column 744.

To quote his views on the matter: "Every soul that leads a righteous life here below necessarily follows Jesus Christ. He is the way,[26] as He Himself teaches. But at the same time He was the first to follow this way. He wants to be our guide and says to all men: 'He who follows Me does not walk in the darkness, but will have the light of life.' [27] And it has pleased Him not to walk alone upon earth, because before Mary sat in glory at His right hand she walked constantly at His side. Therefore, to follow the path that is the Christian life at the present time we must follow this Virgin as well as her divine Son. Like us and going before us, they went to God, the term of their journey. The mysteries were only successive stages of their pilgrimage in this world. These mysteries were their itinerary before they became ours." [28]

Starting with the meditative recitation of the Rosary, with the *Hail Mary* well said, a whole Christian life will spring up, a Marian life, a life of union with Jesus and His beloved Mother. This union with the mysteries of Jesus will extend to the work and apostolate of each day. It will be a union in sanctifying and redemptive suffering. For every Christian life is a life of work, every Christian soul becomes an apostle, and the Christian's every suffering becomes fruitful for the salvation of the world.

This is the fullness of life-giving union with the Word Incarnate and with His divine Mother, embracing the whole existence of Christ's members and making St. Paul's "Christ lives in me" [29] a reality.

---

[26] Cf. John 14:6.  
[27] John 8:12.  
[28] *Les Mystères du Rosaire.*  
[29] Gal. 2:20.

## Texts for Meditation

I was exalted like a cedar in Libanus, and as a cypress tree on Mount Sion.

I was exalted like a palm tree in Cades, and as a rose plant in Jericho:

As a fair olive tree in the plains, and as a plane tree by the water in the streets, was I exalted.

I gave a sweet smell like cinnamon, and aromatical balm: I yielded a sweet odor like the best myrrh:

And I perfumed my dwelling as storax, and galbanum, and onyx, and aloes, and as the frankincense not cut, and my odor is as the purest balm.

I have stretched out my branches as the turpentine tree, and my branches are of honor and grace.

As the vine I have brought forth a pleasant odor; and my flowers are the fruit of honor and riches.

I am the mother of fair love, and of fear, and of knowledge, and of holy hope.

In me is all grace of the way and of the truth, in me is all hope of life, and of virtue.

Come over to me, all ye that desire me, and be filled with my fruits.

For my spirit is sweet above honey, and my inheritance above honey and the honeycomb.

My memory is unto everlasting generations.

They that eat me, shall yet hunger: and they that drink me, shall yet thirst.

He that hearkeneth to me, shall not be confounded: and they that work by me, shall not sin. (Ecclus. 24:17-30.)

"But those wander from the path of truth who consider this devotion merely an annoying formula repeated with monotonous sing-song intonation, and refuse it as good only for children and silly women!

In this regard, it is to be noted that both piety and love, though always renewing the same words, do not always repeat the same thing, but always express something new issuing from the intimate sentiment of devotion. And besides, this mode of prayer has the perfume of evangelic simplicity and requires humility of spirit; and if we disdain humility, as the divine Redeemer teaches, it will be impossible for us to enter the heavenly kingdom: "Amen, I say to you, unless you become as little children you shall not enter the kingdom of heaven." (Matt. 18:3.)

Nevertheless, if men in our century, with its derisive pride, refuse the Holy Rosary, there is an innumerable multitude of holy men of every age and every condition who have always held it dear. They have recited it with great devotion, and in every moment they have used it as a powerful weapon to put the demons to flight, to preserve the integrity of life, to acquire virtue more easily, and in a word to attain real peace among men.

Nor are there lacking men famous as to doctrine and wisdom who, although intensely occupied in scientific study and researches, never even for a day fail to pray fervently on bended knee, before the image of the Virgin, in this most pious form.

Thus kings and princes, however burdened with most urgent occupations and affairs, made it their duty to recite the Rosary.

This mystic crown, then, not only is found in and glides through the hands of the poor, but it also is honored by citizens of every social rank. And We do not wish here to pass over in silence the fact that the Blessed Virgin herself, even in our times, has solicitously recommended this manner of prayer, when she appeared and taught it to the innocent girl in the Grotto of Lourdes.

Therefore why should We not hope for every grace if We supplicate our heavenly Mother in this manner with due disposition and holiness? (Pope Pius XI, *In gravescentibus malis,* September, 1937.)

*Hail,* through the Omnipotence of the Father; Hail, through the Wisdom of the Son; Hail, through the Mercy of the Holy Spirit, O most sweet *Mary,* who dost illumine heaven and earth, *full of grace,* and who dost pour it out in its fullness upon all those who love thee!

*The Lord is with thee,* the only Son of God the Father, the only Son of thy virginal heart, thy most sweet friend and spouse.

*Blessed art thou among women,* for thou didst put to flight the curse pronounced against Eve and didst win for men eternal benediction.

*Blessed is the fruit of thy womb,* the Creator and Master of all things, who blesses and sanctifies all things, who unifies and multiplies all things. (St. Mechthild.)

# CHAPTER 12 ✍

# *Living With Christ and His Mother*

"WHATEVER you do in word or in work, do all in the name of the Lord Jesus, giving thanks to God the Father through Him." [1] These words of the Apostle sum up the whole program of the Christian life. The Christian life does not consist only in praying at certain specified times, in uniting ourselves to the sacrifice of Jesus by going to Mass, or in receiving Jesus in Holy Communion, even every day. Christianity demands essentially that our whole life be a homage of adoration and praise, in a spirit of submission and love, to God our Father in union with Jesus, His beloved Son. "Whether you eat or drink, or do anything else, do all for the glory of God." [2]

Nothing is excluded from this work of praise. Even our lowliest actions must sing the glory of God and be integrated into the one great sacrifice that Christ, the Word Incarnate, offers in the name of all creatures to the glory of His Father. The essential work of Christ's whole life was to glorify His Father. When He was about to die, He said: "Father, . . . I have glorified Thee on earth; I have

[1] Col. 3:17.  [2] I Cor. 10:31.

accomplished the work that Thou hast given Me to do." [3]
He went to His immolation to consummate on the Cross
the priestly mission and great work of glorification which
the Father had entrusted to Him at the moment of His
incarnation in the womb of Mary.

It is for us Christians, the members of His Mystical
Body, to continue this praise the glory to the Blessed
Trinity. How can we succeed in doing it? By living our
life of union with Jesus Christ totally, in all its divine
reality; by living with a deep faith that incorporation in
Christ which began with our baptism; by living our Mass
and our Communion. We must let the blood of Jesus circulate in our soul, for His blood is the vehicle of His
divine life. We must let His blood quicken all our acts,
fecundate all our undertakings, and efface all that remains
in us of the "old man" with his concupiscence. To live
the Christian life is to live by Christ, to see all things
through Him by the light of His grace, to love through
His adorable Heart, to pray through His own divine
prayer, to work through Him and for Him in order to
bring the whole world back to Him, to suffer with Him,
and to make up what is wanting to His redemptive
Passion.

But if we are not to remain in the domain of pure theory
and speculation, we must actualize all these in a deep interior life that is permeated by a lively faith and a generous
love. To this end, the soul must know how to die to itself
for Jesus' sake and in union with Him through the grace
of baptism. This is not the work of a single day; it requires sustained effort and constant and ever-renewed
generosity in the face of our inevitable tendency to back-
slide. Christian asceticism maintains all its rights in this

[3] John 17:1, 3–4.

sphere, providing its practice is integrated into the life of union with Jesus, and providing the soul learns to die *with Jesus* and for His love. Afterwards, or rather simultaneously—for these various efforts are mutually related—we must do with Him and in Him everything that God expects of us, accomplishing our humble duties of each day generously, lovingly, and with a view to our final goal. This goal, of course, is the salvation of our brothers, the building up of the total Christ, and the universal reign of God through Christ.

These perspectives should illumine our souls as we perform our daily tasks, for such concepts dignify our work and elevate it to the level of the Redemption. Once again, it is important that our views should not remain in the speculative order. Some persons delude themselves by constructing beautiful theories based on the concepts of baptism, grace, and the Mystical Body, and then do not live by them. The dogmas at the root of our piety must become incarnate in the humble task of the present moment, in obscure sacrifices, in the renouncement of a thousand selfish quests, and in fidelity to what God asks *here and now,* hour by hour, through the obligations of our state of life. That is the touchstone of true love. "Not everyone who says to Me, 'Lord, Lord,' shall enter the kingdom of heaven; but he who does the will of My Father in heaven." [4] Outside of that, there is nothing but illusion.

The soul that is united to Christ will seek to do the will of the Father together with Jesus. Jesus taught us to make God's will the rule of our life: "My food is to do the will of Him who sent Me." [5] He continues to do this will at the present time through His members, realizing through them His Father's plans of love. God's will, accomplished in all

[4] Matt. 7:21.        [5] John 4:34.

things in union with Jesus, must be the mark of our whole
Christian life. Even if it had only this guidepost, the soul
united to Christ would have an unfailing rule of conduct
and an infallible way of holiness. But we must translate
this general view into the details of our Christian life, so
that everything we do is under the influence of the grace
of our vital union with Christ.

In every human life there is a portion devoted to prayer,
that is, a time especially and exclusively given to God and
to spiritual activities. There is also a portion given over to
work in all its forms. There are relations with neighbor
and the exercise of fraternal charity. There is the practice
of the apostolate, which is the normal development and
the highest expression of charity toward our brothers.
Finally, in every man's life there is a portion of suffering,
so often misunderstood and a scandal to so many. And
yet Jesus embraced, ennobled, and sanctified suffering and
endowed it with divine fruitfulness. Every Christian,
whatever his vocation and condition, whether he remains
in the world or in the cloister, whether he is in the whirl-
wind of affairs or engaged in the pursuit of science or
wisdom, must compose his life from these diverse elements, in proportions that will vary greatly in different
cases. We must strive to permeate all our activities and
sufferings with the spirit and love of Christ, vivify them
with His views and intentions, and submit them to the
life-giving influence of His grace.

Prayer is indispensable to every man who senses his essential dependence upon God. Jesus, the divine Teacher,
teaches us to pray and draws us toward His Father by
the movement of His own filial prayer. "Lord, teach us to
pray," [6] the apostles said to Him one day when they had

6 Luke 11:1.

seen Him deep in humble prayer. And the Master taught them a form of prayer whose fullness will nourish our life of prayer forever. This divine prayer is the one that Jesus Himself addressed to His Father and whose diverse elements recur on His lips throughout the Gospels.

*Our Father!* It is an invocation that the divine Master often repeated: Father! My Father! Just Father! Holy Father! [7]

*Thy name!* "I have glorified Thee on earth; . . . I have manifested Thy name to the men whom Thou hast given me out of the world." [8] This was the great occupation of His life on earth, the object of all His desires, and the goal of all His aspirations and prayers.

*Thy kingdom come!* I have come upon earth to establish it among men, and what do I desire but that it be strengthened and extended throughout the world. Does not Jesus' entire teaching pertain to this kingdom of heaven to be established upon earth? [9]

*Thy will be done,* not Mine! [10] This was His prayer in the Garden, the prayer which prepared Him for the great combat of His passion. It is the prayer He wants us to repeat after Him.

*Our daily bread.* He asked for it for our sakes and prepared it for us at the same time, by teaching us that we must not worry about it but that our first concern must be for the kingdom of God and His justice. [11] He has obtained it for us and given it to us, as far as our souls' nourishment is concerned, by instituting the Sacrament of the altar. [12]

*Forgiveness.* This was His prayer even from the Cross:

---

[7] Cf. Matt. 11:26; Luke 23:46; John 17:1, 11, 24, 25.
[8] John 17:4, 6.     [9] Cf. Matt. 3:2, 4:17; 13:24; John 18:37; etc.
[10] Cf. Matt. 26:42.     [11] Matt. 6:25-33.     [12] Cf. John 6:28-59.

"Father, forgive them, for they do not know what they are doing." [13] Obviously He did not need to make any such request for Himself, but because of the generous pardon He sought for and granted to His executioners, He has given us confidence to seek forgiveness in our turn.

*Lead us not into temptation.* This was Jesus' recommendation in the Garden of Gethsemani: "Watch and pray, that you may not enter into temptation." [14] When we repeat this request after Him, we more readily remember that we must be on our guard.

And finally, *deliver us from evil.* The work of His life was to forewarn us against the evil from which we ask to be delivered. Such is the meaning of His prayer to the Father on behalf of His disciples on Holy Thursday evening: "Holy Father, . . . I do not pray that Thou take them out of the world, but that Thou keep them from evil." [15]

Such is the divine economy of the Lord's prayer. We shall find it much easier and sweeter to recite it after Him when we enter into His great intentions, rely upon His merits, and pray through His Spirit, for the Spirit of Jesus St. Paul tells us, was sent into our hearts "crying, 'Abba, Father.' " [16] If we make the *Our Father* the supreme form of our prayer, all our other prayers will be cast in the same mold. Then we shall pray with the lips and the heart of our great Advocate who, even now that He is in heaven, "lives always to make intercession" [17] for us.

From the moment the Christian awakens in the morning, he unites himself to the prayer of Jesus to call down upon all his actions, thoughts, desires, words, and even his slightest movements the sanctifying power of Christ

---

[13] Luke 23:34.          [14] Matt. 26:41.          [15] John 17:11, 15.
[16] Gal. 4:6.            [17] Heb. 7:25.

and the divine dew of His precious blood which, as St. Thomas says, is the sole cause of all sanctification.[18] Likewise in his mental prayer (if he is wise enough to assure himself this precious consolation) and above all in his prayer of silence, he prays with Jesus, unites himself to Jesus, and finds his support in the mysteries of His sacred humanity.

These are the mysteries that will most often provide him with the theme of his meditations. At times, after he has drawn the substantial fruit from one or another mystery, he will remain united to God, simply looking at Him with faith and love. Even so, the humanity of Christ will still be his fulcrum and his way to the Father, though he may not always be conscious of it. Did not St. Teresa of Avila tell us, in her autobiography, how deeply she regretted having sought for a time to go directly to God without passing through Christ's humanity? [19]

Made strong by his prayer and rich through the divine blood he has received in the morning, the Christian will give himself to his daily occupations in this same spirit of union with Jesus Christ. "Lord, in union with the same divine intention." He can slightly transpose this prayer, which precedes the various hours of the Divine Office, and say: "In union with the holy intention that You had in the fulfillment of Your divine work, I shall at this moment acquit myself of mine."

[18] Cf. *Summa theol.* IIIa, q. 60, a. 3, obj. 2.
[19] We have no intention of condemning all mental prayer in which the soul does not actually call to mind the sacred humanity of Christ. Actual consideration of His humanity may be absent from much mystical contemplation, but either before or after mental prayer, the Christian soul—in its movement toward God—turns to Jesus as the source of every grace and the principle of all true union.

The worker of Nazareth has sanctified the lowly work of the hands. By His sweat and exhaustion the carpenter's Son rehabilitated man's toil, which paganism had degraded to drudgery. Man was enslaved to his work; Christ the Redeemer made him free. He began the Redemption of man in Joseph's workshop, making His own work and that of His brothers a human and Christian activity and, therefore, a divine one. When man, as the true king of creation, dominates the forces of nature and the energies of matter, he makes them serve his own perfection and the glory of the divine Creator.

"Far from imprisoning himself in his own techniques, he invents his means and instruments only to realize his spiritual aims. The Christian engaged in such labor seeks to release the energies and riches of nature, to rid the earth of thorns and briars, to penetrate it with intelligible intentions and results, and thus make all things sing together. Toil of the husbandman, . . . toil of the engineer, . . . toil of the scientist, . . . all are so many efforts to humanize the universe and to make it better than it was even in God's eyes." [20]

O that man, with his terrible power to sin, would not subject this material world to his perverse ends, as too often happens! Did not St. Paul tell us: "We know that all creation groans and travails in pain until now"? [21] The reason for this is that instead of serving to glorify God, according to its natural capacities and through its usefulness to man, "creation was made subject to vanity—not by its own will but by reason of Him who made it subject —in hope, because creation itself also will be delivered

[20] Jean Mouroux, *The Meaning of Man* (New York: Sheed & Ward, 1948), p. 28.
[21] Rom. 8:22.

from its slavery to corruption into the freedom of the glory of the sons of God." [22]

The redemption of the universe is effected through Christ, as Mouroux tells us: "Christ came, and the whole world was redeemed. By His incarnation—in which God took a human soul and body and became man like ourselves—He entered into union with all the most spiritual and also with all the most carnal elements of the universe. As sin had thrown everything out of joint, so the coming of God in the flesh brought everything renewal and healing. God's benediction, made present and active in Christ, restored the divine face of men and things and gave them back their spiritual meaning." [23]

Man's labors, ennobled and sanctified by the grace of Christ, have the mission to accomplish this redemption. The purpose of man's work is to redirect every creature to its noble purpose, to make of every creature a step leading to God, and to make creation as a whole a pure and harmonious song of glory to the Creator. This spirit of restoring the dignity of labor, whether in factories or on farms, inspires Catholic Action groups and other organizations for the rehabilitation of the working man. It is a spirit that becomes incarnate in the creative effort of each day, but which also finds expression in the catchwords, ardent prayers, and fraternal help of worker to worker. "Because it produces the useful and the beautiful, work is admirably human, and it is not in the least surprising to see it give birth to a practical mystique in which intelligent energy, industrious courage, and a consuming passion for efficiency can all be employed to the full." [24]

[22] *Ibid.*, 8:20–21.     [23] Mouroux, *op. cit.*, p. 25.
[24] Mouroux, *op. cit.*, p. 28. This mysticism of work had already found expression in the beautiful verses of Paul Vrignault, the nineteenth-century poet of the working man.

All these movements have their source in the work of
the docile Apprentice, the divine Worker of Nazareth.
When He took carpenter's tools into His divine hands, He
restored to human labor its original integrity. In fact, He
raised it infinitely higher, by His grace as the God-man
who represents and completes the work of creation. Man
will sanctify his own work by uniting it, in faith and love,
to the work of Christ. In this way he will give his labor
nobility, grandeur, and redemptive value and will accomplish the work of redeeming his brothers in union with
the divine Savior.

After work, rest. Rest also needs to be sanctified and
quickened by Christ. The divine Master knew how to give
His exhausted body the relaxation it needed after a day's
work. There is great consolation for us in the Gospel scenes
in which Jesus, so much one of us in His humanity, allowed His human nature the refreshment demanded by
His weakened physical strength. "Jesus, therefore, wearied
as He was from the journey, was sitting at [Jacob's] well." [25]
It was about noon, the sun's heat added to his exhaustion.
It was in Samaria, where Jesus was to use His period of
rest to evangelize the Samaritan woman and her fellow
countrymen.

Jesus also needed sleep, that common weakness of our
nature. True, the Gospel often shows Him to us spending
nights in prayer, as the divine model of so many monks
and saints who were to devote these silent hours to recollection in God. But we also know that He allowed Himself
to become drowsy and that He slept during the raging
storm on the Sea of Galilee. But even during sleep He
maintained mastery over His acts and the power to command and control nature. When His terrified apostles
awoke Him with the cry: "Master, we are perishing!" He

[25] John 4:6.

replied with assurance and with a suggestion of reproach: "Where is your faith?" [26]

We should not forget that Jesus' weaknesses were not the same as ours. They were really "divine weaknesses," possessing the power that proceeds from everything that belongs to Christ and His sacred humanity. These weaknesses, therefore, had more power to save us than all the strength of creatures. But after all, is this not the law of the Incarnation? Christ snatched us from death by succumbing to it Himself, and all His sufferings, including the scandal of His passion, became the instrument of the power of God to raise up fallen humanity and to break the bonds of sin. In the words of St. Paul: "The weakness of God is stronger than men." [27]

Jesus experienced our weaknesses in order to have compassion upon His brothers, as the Apostle informs us.[28] And so the divine Master provided for His apostles, no less than for Himself, the necessary rest from their apostolic labors. "Come apart into a desert place and rest a while," [29] He said to His apostles after one of their missionary journeys. For, as St. Mark notes, they did not even have time to eat, so great was the demand of the crowds. There is deep wisdom in Jesus' thoroughly human behavior in this matter. It poses the principle of the sanctification of leisure, which is of great concern to those who want to procure for the working man more humane living conditions that favor the development of his spiritual life. All who have tried to provide honorable recreation and wholesome pleasures for the workers—St. John Bosco, Timon-David, Jean Le Provost, Maurice Maignen, and the rest—are true disciples of the divine Master.

Joy is another of Christ's gifts to the world, and the

---

[26] Cf. Luke 8:24–25.
[28] Cf. Heb. 2:17; 4:15.

[27] I Cor. 1:25.
[29] Mark 6:31.

true life of union with Jesus develops in an atmosphere of joy. For God is eternal joy, and the vocation He has given us is to share in the fullness of His joy. To the faithful servant He will say: "Enter into the joy of thy Master." [30] And the angels' message to the shepherds of Bethlehem was a message of "great joy." [31]

In the present fallen and sinful state of man, the Christian can win eternal happiness only by expiatory suffering and pain in union with Christ. Later we shall discuss the salutary role of suffering endured for love and in accordance with God's will. But even here on earth Jesus gives His disciples an interior peace and joy whose secret the world cannot understand.[32] And the Apostle attested to the truth of the Master's words: "I overflow with joy in all our troubles." [33]

The whole life of Jesus upon earth was a mystery of intertwined joy and sorrow. Even during His passion, when His soul was plunged in a sea of bitterness, He still enjoyed in the upper reaches of His soul the ineffable joy of the beatific vision. And His disciples' joy is simply a participation of His own. As He told them before He went to Calvary: "These things I have spoken to you that My joy may be in you, and that your joy may be made full." [34]

How can the Christian who has faith fail to live in this atmosphere of joy? It is the joy of knowing that God is infinitely great, good, perfect, and happy; the joy of knowing that through union with Christ the soul possesses the pledge of future happiness. As Father Bernadot writes: "The fundamental joy for the Christian is to know that God is. God exists! The Infinite. Essential and necessary being. The cause of all—truth, beauty, goodness, benevo-

---

[30] Matt. 25:23.    [31] Luke 2:10.    [32] Cf. John 14:27.
[33] II Cor. 7:4.    [34] John 15:11; cf. also John 17:13.

lence, power, holiness, sovereign purity, justice, and love.
. . . God exists! He is all that! He is that eternally, un-
changeably, infinitely!" [35]

And the mystery of the Trinity: the Father, the Word
who is the splendor of His glory, and the Holy Ghost who
is the term of Their mutual love! "To know this is a source
of supreme and unending joy for the loving soul." [36] And
the object of our joy dwells within us! Father Bernadot
continues: "The source of all joy is in us: 'He who believes
in Me, . . . from within him there shall flow rivers of
living water.' And the Evangelist adds: '[Jesus] said this,
however, of the Spirit whom they who believed in Him
were to receive.' (John 7:38–39)." [37] Baptism has opened
up this interior wellspring, and each time we go to Holy
Communion, the stream becomes deeper and broader.
"The stream of the river maketh the city of God joyful:
the most High hath sanctified His own tabernacle." [38]
The slightest truth of faith is a world of joy in which our
soul can find delight at every moment. In the words of St.
Peter: "Yet believing, you exult with a joy unspeakable
and triumphant." [39]

We can therefore understand why the Apostle urges the
faithful to live in continual joy: "Rejoice in the Lord
always; again I say, rejoice." [40] Who can dry up this fountain of holy joy within us, since, according to the Master's
promise, our sorrow will be turned to joy? [41]

The way to preserve this joy, at least in the depths of
our soul—even in moments when we drink the chalice of
the Passion together with Jesus—consists in a communion

[35] M.-V. Bernadot, O.P., *From Holy Communion to the Blessed
Trinity*, translated by Dom Francis Izard, O.S.B. (Westminster, Md.:
The Newman Press, 1952), pp. 87–88.

[36] *Ibid.*, p. 88.      [37] *Ibid.*, p. 89.      [38] Ps. 45:5.

[39] I Pet. 1:8.      [40] Phil. 4:4.      [41] Cf. John 16:20.

of every instant with Him in His life and in His mysteries. Now that we are approaching the end of our study, we must repeat what we said in the beginning: all grace, all holiness, all possession of God and of His divine joy come to us through Christ's life-giving humanity, and we can apply to this humanity the words of the Book of Wisdom: "All good things came to me together with her." [42]

Treasures of holiness and the riches of divine life can spring forth from the least of our acts, if they are united to the theandric activity of the Word Incarnate, to the divine-and-human operations of His most sacred humanity. But we can obtain this result only in the measure that we are informed about this mystery of life, this great mystery of Christ. That is why St. Paul's chief concern throughout his apostolate, as he told the Philippians, was: "That your charity may more and more abound in knowledge and all discernment, so that you may approve the better things, that you may be upright and without offense unto the day of Christ, filled with the fruit of justice [works of holiness], through Jesus Christ, to the glory and praise of God." [43]

Our union with Jesus is completed and extended through our close union with His Mother. As St. Pius X has said: "From Nazareth to Calvary was she not the constant companion of Jesus?" [44] Mary is the eminent model of the life of union with Christ the Redeemer. She penetrated the mysteries and the most secret intentions of the Heart of Jesus in each of His sacred actions. Hence, if we unite ourselves to Mary, we are united ourselves to Christ; if we rest upon our Mother's heart, we sense the heartbeats of her divine Son. This devotion, at once Christian and

[42] Wisd. 7:11.                    [43] Phil. 1:9–11.
[44] Encyclical *Ad diem illum.*

Marian, finds beautiful expression in the following couplets by St. Louis-Marie de Montfort:

> It is You alone whom I adore,
> Heart of my God, glorious Heart;
> But when I adore You I honor
> The Heart of the Queen of heaven.

> Christians, through the heart of Mary
> We love the Heart of Jesus,
> For Jesus began His life
> In her heart and in her virtues.

The union between Jesus and Mary began in the mystery of the divine maternity and was consummated in the mystical compenetration of soul and sentiment between Christ and His Mother. It was the perfect fulfillment of the *Cor unum et anima una* (one heart and one soul), so well presented in another of Montfort's stanzas:

> From the blood of her heart afire
> The Heart of Jesus was formed;
> They have but one heart and soul,
> Both of them must be loved.

Inasmuch as Mary is totally transformed into the likeness of Jesus, she herself will initiate us into the secrets of His divine heart. By her example alone she will help to reproduce in us Jesus' way of being and acting, which will make us true Christians. Actually, there are certain aspects of the Christian life that only the Blessed Virgin can teach us. I am thinking in particular of Mary's faith, which St. Louis-Marie exalts so often in his Treatise on the *True Devotion to the Blessed Virgin.*[45]

Since Jesus always saw His Father face to face, He could

[45] Cf. particularly no. 214.

not have faith, and yet His beatific knowledge is the
supreme model and source of our faith, because it is He
who revealed to us the mysteries of God which we believe.
But Mary had faith. And how deep was her faith! As her
cousin Elizabeth told her: "Blessed is she who has believed!" [46] Mary believed with a luminous faith in the
greatest and most unfathomable of God's mysteries: God
present within her, the Son of God incarnate in her
womb.

To quote Father Bernadot: "Our Lady is called *Virgo
fidelis,* the Virgin of faith, by the Church. Faith in the
angel's word, though he announced an ineffable mystery,
admitted her to the mystery of Christ, the mystery which,
as St. Paul says, God had kept hidden from all eternity.
Those secrets of the Trinity, the Incarnation, and the
Mystical Body, how did Mary learn of them but from the
word of God's messenger? 'Blessed art thou who has believed' (Luke 1:45), said her cousin to her. When she had
accepted the message in faith, she entered into the fulfillment of God's greatest designs. The Word would live
in her because of her faith. All her love for her Son rested
on that unshakeable faith which God subjected to such
terrible trials. Her pure, simple faith made her the handmaid of the Lord." [47]

Mary's hidden life in Nazareth was the development of
this faith. The Child who played at her side, the young
Apprentice who worked with Joseph, was God among
men. And Mary's faith held fast to the mystery of the
hidden God who by His slightest action was already saving and sanctifying us, even while He was sanctifying
Mary and Joseph. More than any of the saints who were
to come after them, Mary and Joseph were intimately

[46] Luke 1:45.          [47] *Our Lady in Our Life,* p. 128.

united to Christ's life-giving humanity in which "dwells all the fullness of the Godhead bodily." [48]

Mary's faith remained serene even during the anguish of the Passion. In the mangled body of her Son, she saw the majesty of God abased, Him whom the penitent thief confessed and the Roman centurion proclaimed to be the son of God.[49]

United to Jesus by her luminous faith, Mary shared in the intentions of His divine heart. It is an easy matter to establish the parallels between the attitudes of Jesus and those of His Mother. The words of Christ which express His state of soul from the moment of His coming into the world are these: "Behold, I come . . . to do Thy will, O God." [50] And Mary's words, which echo her Son's, are contained in her answer to the angel: "Behold the handmaid of the Lord." [51]

The law of Christ's conduct throughout His earthly life was to do the will of His Father. To His every command and desire, He answered: "Thy will be done!" [52] Mary expressed her obedience to the divine will by saying: "Be it done to me according to thy word." [53] Jesus gave the same rule of perfection to His disciples: "If anyone love Me, he will keep My word." [54] And at Cana, His Mother gave similar advice: "Do whatever He tells you." [55] When He was about to die, Jesus evaluated His mortal life with the words: "Father, . . . I have glorified Thee." [56] And when His Blessed Mother was praised, she referred all her glory to God: "My soul magnifies the Lord!" [57]

Clearly, the essential lines of these two lives converged,

[48] Col. 2:9.  [49] Cf. Matt. 27:54.  [50] Heb. 10:7.
[51] Luke 1:38.  [52] Matt. 26:42.  [53] Luke 1:38.
[54] John 14:23.  [55] John 2:5.  [56] John 17:1; 4.
[57] Luke 1:46.

to the point of meeting in a single line. From the moment of the Annunciation, the lives of Jesus and Mary were fused into a single life. And Mary's soul, which was united to that of her Son a thousand times more closely than Jonathan's was united to David's,[58] embraced all His sentiments, shared all His virtuous intentions, and lived all His mysteries inwardly.

That is why the Christian soul goes so easily from Jesus to Mary or from Mary to Jesus. Sometimes, under the inspiration of the Holy Spirit, it unites itself to Christ, seeking to reproduce His virtues and divine states; at other times it unites itself to His Mother, to be formed by her and in her to the likeness of her Son. From this, St. Louis-Marie concludes: "If Mary, who is the tree of life, is well cultivated in our soul, . . . she will bear her fruit in her own time, and her fruit is none other than Jesus Christ." [59]

May she guide us on the paths that Jesus followed. May she share with us the grace of Christ, the fullness of which she received.[60] May she grant us some part of the superabundant life that her Son came upon earth to bring,[61] so that we may follow her example and be filled, each according to his own measure, "unto all the fullness of God." [62]

### TEXTS FOR MEDITATION

Put on therefore, as God's chosen ones, holy and beloved, a heart of mercy, kindness, humility, meekness, patience. Bear with one another and forgive one another, if anyone has a grievance against any other; even as the Lord has forgiven you, so also do you forgive.

---

[58] Cf. I Kings 18:1.                    [59] *True Devotion*, p. 194.
[60] Cf. Luke 1:28.        [61] Cf. John 10:10.        [62] Eph. 3:19.

But above all these things have charity, which is the bond of perfection. And may the peace of Christ reign in your hearts; unto that peace, indeed, you were called in one body.

Show yourselves thankful.

Let the word of Christ dwell in you abundantly: in all wisdom teach and admonish one another by psalms, hymns and spiritual songs, singing in your hearts to God by His grace.

Whatever you do in word or in work, do all in the name of the Lord Jesus, giving thanks to God the Father through Him. (Col. 3:12-17.)

We must train ourselves to look at Jesus in all things and to have no other object in all our exercises of devotion and in all our actions except Him and all His states, mysteries, virtues, and actions. For He is wholly in all things: He is the being of things that are, the life of living things, the beauty of beautiful things, the power of the powerful, the wisdom of the wise, the virtue of the virtuous, the holiness of the saints.

There is scarcely anything we do but that He did something similar while He was on earth. And it is His actions that we must look at and imitate when we perform our own. By so doing we shall fill our thoughts with Jesus, and we shall form and establish Jesus in our mind, for we shall think of Him often and fix our eyes upon Him in all things.

Not only must we form Jesus in our mind by thinking about Him and looking at Him in all things. We must also form Him in our heart by the frequent exercise of His divine love. To this end, we must accustom ourselves to raise our heart often toward Him through love, to do all our actions purely for love of Him, to consecrate all the affections of our heart to Him.

We must form Jesus within us by a total annihilation of ourselves and of all things in us. For if we want Jesus to live and reign perfectly in us, we must kill and annihilate all creatures in our mind and heart, and not look at them or love them in themselves, but in Jesus, and Jesus in them. (St. John Eudes.)

Henceforth, you must not have a will of your own. Put Me in the place of your will, so that I may act through you. When you work, I work through you; when you rest, I rest within you; in a word, in all that you do, it must no longer be you but I. I see with your eyes, I work with your hands, I speak with your lips, I pray through you.

And since My greatest desire was to suffer constantly, I shall suffer again in you and through you. Dispose yourself, therefore, and be ready to suffer. I thus continue My Passion, and I apply it to souls by suffering through My chosen ones. (Mother Marie du Divin Cœur.)


I adore You, O my divine Jesus, dwelling and living in the Most Blessed Virgin.

I adore Your grandeurs and perfections, which adorn her soul.

I adore Your reign over her, and the absolute power that rules her whole being.

I adore Your life, that fills and quickens her heart and all her powers.

I adore the abundance of the gifts, the fullness of the virtues, and the fruitfulness of the graces that You place in her for Your whole Church.

Divine Jesus, reign in her, and through her in us, forever!

Divine Lord, Your power is adorable, and Your reign is always gentle; but it is never more gentle than upon this throne of love.

Let us eagerly come to the feet of this holy tabernacle, to render our duties to You and to beseech You to destroy in us whatever is opposed to Your life!

Divine Jesus, quicken our hearts! Do not suffer any life in us except Your own! Destroy and annihilate all that is contrary to it! Act within us as You do within Your Mother: may You be the only one to live in us, and may all that is mortal in us be absorbed in Your life! (Father Olier.)

# CHAPTER 13 ✍

# *Fraternal Charity and the Apostolate*

"THAT all may be one, even as Thou, Father, in Me and I in Thee; that they also may be one in us!" [1] Such was Jesus' supreme prayer for those whom He had united to Himself, like branches to the vine. [2] The divine life that He infused into them was the same that He had drawn from the bosom of the Father, [3] and would now become for His disciples a ferment of charity and a principle of unity. Unity in God, charity for our brothers: this is the life of Christ in us, for when we love our brothers, it is He, the most loving Master, who loves them in us.

Our brothers! The whole supernatural life brings us back to them. Man, Christian man, does not live an isolated life. Even if he is a recluse and separated from the world by his vocation, he remains bound to the human race by multiple ties. And those who are most completely separated, those who are cloistered, are sometimes—not to say always—those who through a grace of spiritual fruitfulness act most efficaciously on the destiny of their brethren.

[1] John 17:21.    [2] Cf. *Ibid.,* 15:1–10.
[3] Cf. I John 1:2–3.

We need only call to mind the example of a Charles de Foucauld, of the recently canonized St. Nicholas of Flüe, and on a larger scale, the truly prodigious case of the little nun buried in an unknown Carmel of Normandy who is now invoked throughout the world as St. Thérèse of the Child Jesus.

Our relationships with our neighbor, which make up a great portion of life, will become Christian relationships: Christian in their inspiration, Christian by their influence and their finality. They will be Christian in both respects if they obey the impulse of fraternal charity. Charity, the love of our brothers in Christ and for Christ's sake, constitutes the great law of our relationships with our neighbor. It is likewise, as Jesus has told us, the most manifest sign of our life in Christ: "By this will all men know that you are My disciples, if you have love for one another." [4]

Why did our Lord place so much stress on the practice of charity? Because, according to Jesus, to love our neighbor is to love Christ Himself. "Amen I say to you, as long as you did it for one of these, the least of My brethren, you did it for Me." [5] Our neighbor is a member of Christ, or else—if he does not yet have this joy—he can become one through the very exercise of our charity. How can we live by Christ without loving Him in the person of our brother? How can we love Jesus without loving those whom He loves? It follows that an authentic Christian life must distinguish itself by its profound, delicate, efficacious, and helpful charity for neighbor.

Fraternal charity shows itself in many ways and bears many fruits. Highest and first in the order of intention is the desire and the efficacious will to obtain for our

[4] John 13:35.                    [5] Matt. 25:40.

neighbor the one and only good that really matters, what ever he himself may think: the possession of God, God known and loved. Without this, our charity would degenerate into sterile philanthropy. In the words of Dom Marmion: "To love our neighbor supernaturally is, indeed, to love him in view of God, to the end that he may gain or preserve God's grace which will bring him to eternal beatitude. To love is to 'wish good' to another, says St. Thomas, but all individual good is subordinate to the supreme good. That is why to give God, the Infinite Good, to the ignorant by instructing them, is so pleasing to God; and so is it to pray for the conversion of infidels and sinners that they may receive the faith or recover divine grace." [6]

It is true that often the first revelation of God we make to our straying brothers is through the corporal works of mercy. Many souls that were closed to Christ's message and prejudiced against priests have recognized Jesus "in the breaking of the bread." [7] They have discovered the God of love hidden in the humble services of a Daughter of Charity or a Little Sister of the Poor. As Father Boulard points out: "The great revelation of Christianity is its incarnation in our daily life. [Jesus has said:] 'Even so let your light shine before men, in order that they may see your good works and give glory to your Father in heaven.'" [8] This law of charity is abundantly verified in fact, as can be seen in the following incident, which I cite from memory.

A workman's wife and the mother of a family fell ill. There was no one to take care of the children or manage the home. The mother wanted to ask the Little Sisters of

[6] *Christ the Life of the Soul,* p. 337.    [7] Luke 24:35.
[8] *Problèmes missionnaires de la France rurale* (Paris, 1945).

the Assumption, who ministered in the neighborhood, to help her. "Never!" was her husband's angry answer. But the illness dragged on, the children were not cared for, and there was only cold, unpalatable food to eat. Something had to be done. The woman timidly repeated her earlier suggestion that they send for a Little Sister. "You can see for yourself," she said, "that we have no choice."

"All right, but be sure I never meet her!"

And so it was arranged. The Little Sister, like an angel of mercy, took up her charitable duties day after day. In the morning, after the father had gone, she would quietly get to work with a smile. The children were dressed, washed, and combed; the sick woman was given the best of care; the house was swept, cleaned, and set in order as perhaps never before. Above all, the cooking was done with real artistry. The husband could not help noticing all this, but true to his promise, he never came in until after the Sister had left.

However, his prejudices were beginning to crumble as a result of the favorable changes in his little home. His wife and children were always telling him about the kindnesses of the Little Sister. But he had vowed he would not see her! He had practically pledged himself to this in the presence of some of his fellow-workers.

One day the menu included a particularly succulent rabbit. It must have been a special feast day. The man did honor to the banquet, as did all the children and their mother, who was rapidly regaining strength. He decided that the least he could do was thank the wonderful cook. After all, he didn't want to be a boor! It was just too bad about his comrades. Wasn't he master in his own house? And having argued himself into this position, he decided to wait until the Little Sister returned. His meeting with

her completed his change of heart. The Sister soon put
him at ease by her simplicity and unassuming kindliness.
His old prejudices against sisters and priests collapsed.
The ice had been broken. He spoke to her and listened
to her speak, and found himself unconsciously transported
on the wings of divine charity into a new world that was
very different from the atmosphere of hate in which he
had been living. From then on he no longer waited until
the Sister had left. By degrees, he felt he was a better man,
rising toward the light. He made contacts at his church.
Soon, he and his whole household approached the One
who had inspired so much self-sacrifice and generosity.
The truth had entered his soul by the door of his heart.

This is what every Christian, united to Jesus by charity,
must accomplish throughout his life. He must give love
in order to harvest souls! He must radiate joy, and so win
hearts to Christ. To quote Dom Marmion: "Christ loved
to give pleasure. The first miracle of His public life was
to change water into wine at the marriage feast of Cana,
so as to spare His hosts any confusion when the wine
failed.[9] We hear Him promise to refresh all who labor and
are burdened and come to Him.[10] And how well He has
kept His promise! The Evangelists often repeat that it is
because He is moved with compassion [11] that He works
His miracles; it is from this motive He cures the lepers and
raises the son of the widow of Naim. . . . Christ, says St.
Paul, . . . is the very kindness of God appearing upon
earth; [12] He is a King, but a King full of meekness,[13] who
bids us forgive and proclaims those blessed who, following
His example, are merciful." [14]

[9] Cf. John 2:1–11.    [10] Cf. Matt. 11:28.
[11] Cf. Luke 7:13.    [12] Cf. Titus 3:4.    [13] Cf. Matt. 21:5.
[14] Cf. Matt. 5:7. *Christ the Life of the Soul,* pp. 337–338.

That is how the divine Savior showed Himself to men, as "He went about doing good and healing." [15] And that is how His disciples must show themselves: "This is My commandment, that you love one another as I have loved you." [16] We must spare no effort to enter into this spirit of Christ. To succeed, we shall have to trample underfoot our self-love, pay little heed to our sensibilities, and swallow every insult in silence, like our Master who endured the unkindness of His apostles and shielded with His merciful silence the shame of the poor sinful woman whom the Pharisees, through want of love, had berated in His presence. The rigor of justice does not suffice to assure harmony between brothers. We should keep in mind a charming remark of St. Thérèse: "God has not established us as justices of the peace, but as angels of peace." [17] "Blessed are the peacemakers!" [18] They shall be the children of God and the messengers of Christ who has left us His peace.

The exercise of charity as a continuation of Christ's vast love for us is an apostolate that springs forth spontaneously from every Christian life, from all true union with Jesus. As Dom Marmion has told us: the first concern of a soul that loves its neighbor is to give God to him. Antoinette de Geuser has said admirably: "The love with which He has set me afire has for a long time kept me consummated in the unity of the Trinity. But there the fire of my love rages so wildly that, without losing its serenity, it clamors for something else. It needs to give! Yes, because I love my God, I want to bring souls to Him; because I love souls, I want to bring them to God. . . .

[15] Acts 10:38.                              [16] John 15:12.

[17] Cf. *Saint Thérèse of Lisieux, the Little Flower of Jesus* (New York: P. J. Kenedy, 1927), p. 313.

[18] Matt. 5:9.

Others do not attract me; it is He who impels me toward them. I must share my riches with them without leaving God's bosom. Practically speaking, I want to strive more than ever to sanctify myself by the intensity of my love, in His good pleasure, for His greater glory. That is the best means of accumulating the material for a beautiful apostolic career." [19]

There are many ways of realizing this conquest of souls. There is first of all the hidden apostolate of a deep interior life, which is mysteriously efficacious in virtue of the communion of saints. Such is the apostolate of the cloistered in their holy solitude, who, through love and generous immolation call down graces of salvation upon the materialistic world. It is also the apostolate of certain unknown souls living in the world and with whom we rub elbows in our daily life without even guessing who they are. But in the end their power and influence finally burst forth for all to see. There are untold marvels of grace in this order of activity, the secret of which we shall learn only on judgment day. And yet while this apostolate of the interior life belongs in a special way to those who live apart from the world, it is not their exclusive privilege. All true apostles must have it to a greater or less degree. For the fact remains that in order to diffuse life we must possess it ourselves. It is still true that the interior life is the soul of the apostolate.

There is also the apostolate of example. "Even so let your light shine before men, in order that they may see your good works and give glory to your Father in heaven." [20] The apostolate of example; and not only the

---

[19] Quoted by Raoul Plus, S.J., in *Consummata,* translated by George Baker (New York: Benziger, 1931).
[20] Matt. 5:16.

example of religious practice. This is necessary, but it must
extend to all the actions of an authentic Christian life. Too
often, frequent attendance at Mass and reception of the
sacraments are contradicted by a life that is not ruled by
the spirit of Christ and becomes a stumbling block for
nonchurchgoers.[21] What Jesus and the Church expect of
us is the example of effective Christianity. They want us
to reveal the efficacy and fruitfulness of our sacramental
and liturgical life in our external conduct by the practice
of charity and justice and by fidelity to all the duties of our
family and social life.

The Christian united to Christ needs a living and effective faith. St. James asks: "What will it profit, . . .
if a man says he has faith, but does not have works?" And
he gives a concrete example of what he means: "If a brother
or a sister be naked and in want of daily food, and one
of you say to them, 'Go in peace, be warmed and filled';
and yet you do not give them what is necessary for the body,
what does it profit? So faith too, unless it has works, is
dead in itself." [22]

If this sterile faith is dead in itself, it will not give life
to others nor will it win the souls of our brothers. The
apostolate of example, therefore, is the example of a

[21] Father Boulard gives us an example of this in his study,
*Problèmes missionnaires de la France rurale:* "At X, the church is
well kept. In addition to the Sisters, there are two old maiden
ladies who run a dry goods store in the village and devote themselves
to the upkeep of the church, the flowers, the altars . . . The other
day they rather shocked one of their customers. They were demand-
ing a really exorbitant price for the material they were selling her.
The customer protested: 'It seems to me that for good Christian
ladies you sell your merchandise quite high.' And the two good
ladies gave the astonishing answer: 'Oh! business has nothing to do
with religion.' "

[22] James 2:14–17.

sincere Christian life, in church and outside of church, within the home and on the public square, at work and at play, in the factory or behind the counter. In all these circumstances and in a thousand others the Christian must reveal to the world that he bears within him a superior principle of life, a rule of righteousness and loyalty, a desire for justice and charity that govern all his conduct. Then he will have the right to speak and propose to others his ideal of perfection and to draw them to Christ, who already shines through his own life.

There is likewise an apostolate of word and action for everyone without exception, an apostolate that is more urgent today than ever before. Like all apostolic action, it flows from our union with Jesus and from our practical and vital understanding of the great mystery of the total Christ, in which all the members of the Mystical Body are united as one and react upon one another either for good or for evil. As Father Plus writes:

"The deeper a soul's realization of the mysteries of Christ, the more readily is she drawn toward apostolic work, and the greater her zeal for it, the more important is it for her to learn about Christ. 'You must understand,' said our Lord to a Poor Clare,[23] 'that the sufferings of My heart were without number. . . . I am the Head of the body and all Christians are the members, and many of them are and will be snatched from Me by mortal sin.'

"These multiple sufferings of the divine Head are a great grief to the soul who has remained a faithful member of His Mystical Body. Lord, have pity on all these members who have gone astray; on them and on us have mercy. I want to glorify Thee, but not alone; to love Thee and embrace Thee, but in company with others. To love

[23] Blessed Baptista Varani.

God is to have the wish that all men should love Him. By my prayers, exhortations, and tactful explanations, I want to bring Thee as many members as possible, so that all men, joined in one splended union, may sing their *Magnificat.*" [24]

That is our divine Master's own way, and how necessary it is! It makes use of every available resource, fashions an arrow out of every piece of wood, and is ever on the watch for an occasion to bring souls closer to God. "Provided only that in every way . . . Christ is being proclaimed!" [25] to use the Apostle's words. There are many human activities that can serve as ways of grace, if carried on under the impulse of a deep love of God and souls. For love always remains the initial motive power, the interior fire that blazes up in flames of zeal. "I have come to cast fire upon the earth, and what will I but that it be kindled?" [26] The apostles must be spreaders of this divine fire, going everywhere, as Montfort says, "with the shining and flaming torch of the Holy Gospel in their mouths and the Holy Rosary in their hands; . . . burning like fires to light up the darkness of the world like suns." [27]

The ways of spreading the kingdom of God are many and varied. They include prayer, the interior life, example, and direct action. To these we must add *the apostolate of suffering.* Such is the law of Providence under the present dispensation. "Without the shedding of blood there is no forgiveness." [28] The salvation of the world was wrought on the Cross, and the Church, the Mystical Body

---

[24] Raoul Plus, S.J., *Christ in His Brethren,* translated by Irene Hernaman (London: Burns Oates and Washbourne Ltd., 1925), pp. 108–109.

[25] Phil. 1:18.                    [26] Luke 12:49.

[27] St. Louis-Marie's prayer asking God for missionaries.

[28] Heb. 9:22.

of Jesus, continues to save men through the power of redemption and life that she draws from the sufferings of her children.

The mystery of suffering! True, many are shocked by it, but there are some whom it attracts. Some try to reject it without success, thus adding the torment of revolt to their suffering. Others submit to it and accept it in the end in a spirit of faith, with a *fiat* of resignation. Finally, others embrace suffering with love, yearn for it ardently, with a holy rapture, and this is the only explanation for the folly of love of the Crucified. Souls that thrill with Jesus in the embrace of the Cross are heroic souls whose vocation is one of reparation, souls that are redemptive by choice and by grace.[29] "I have a baptism [of blood] with which to be baptized; and how distressed I am until it is accomplished!"[30]

The divine impatience to suffer for God and for souls has been echoed in a legion of heroic souls who have aspired—humbly and depending only on God's strength —to carry the Savior's cross and to be crucified with

---

[29] There are beautiful examples of this in Father Plus' work: *The Folly of the Cross* (Westminster, Md.: Newman Press, 1949). But we would caution our readers against an illusion: heroism is not always to be found in an attitude of exaltation and enthusiasm for the cross and suffering. Jesus, our divine Head, experienced weariness and repugnance in the Garden of Gethsemani, but His generous will conquered the repulsion of nature and said *Fiat*. Many saints after Him have experienced the terrors of agony and had only enough strength from minute to minute to suffer as much as was necessary without succumbing. Thus, St. Thérèse of the Child Jesus taught her sister to suffer "weakly," in a sentiment of acquiescence in one's weakness, looking upon this, too, as a part of the suffering. "Oh! how hard it is to give Jesus what He asks! What happiness that it is so hard! What ineffable joy to carry our crosses weakly!" (Letter 59.)

[30] Luke 12:50.

Christ.[31] One of these lovers of the Cross writes in his spiritual notebook: "O sweet joys of suffering! Oh happy isolation of the Cross! But you are understood only by the soul that knows how to love. . . . The strong soul finds its rest in pain; the weak soul experiences the bitterness of pain and loses its peace because of it." [32]

Suffering as a means of apostolic action; Elizabeth Leseur understood it well. Writing to a friend, she said: "Suffering is the superior form of action, the highest expression of the admirable communion of saints." [33] She continues: "I know what suffering represents, the admirable and mysterious power that it possesses, what it obtains and what it accomplishes. In reality, our action [which we owe to God and to others], is a very small thing and is exercised only in the measure that Providence deigns to dispose of it. Therefore, when Providence is pleased to make use of suffering to accomplish an undertaking, I think we should not complain too much, for then we are sure that the task will be well done and that it will be free of all the flaws of selfishness and pride that sometimes sadly mar our exterior activity."

This is the language of all who understand the mystery of Christ and His Redemption. Dom Marmion says in one of his letters: "Sufferings are the sign and the price of true divine favors. Only the works and foundations built on the cross and on suffering endure." [34]

St. Margaret Mary says: "I see nothing that so mitigates

[31] Cf. Gal. 2:19.

[32] Dom Pius de Hemptinne, quoted in Dom Thibaut's *Un Disciple de Dom Marmion.*

[33] *Elizabeth Leseur*, p. 24.

[34] Quoted in Dom Thibaut's *L'Union à Dieu d'après les lettres de direction de Dom Marmion* (Paris: Desclée de Brouwer, 1934), p. 258.

the length of life as constantly to suffer for the sake of love." But she wisely adds a remark that we should remember: "This does not mean that we should ask for suffering, for it is more perfect to ask nothing and to refuse nothing." It is more perfect and it is also more prudent, in order to avoid any foolhardy presumption or dangerous illusion.

At any rate, God does not fail to satisfy the holy desires for suffering that He finds in generous souls. The Christian soul conscious of its Christianity is given ample occasion to unite its host to the sacrifice of Calvary and to renew its offering each day with Jesus immolated on the altar. To name but a few of these providential crosses that usually do not end until we die, there are illnesses, interior trials, painful struggles against the ill-will of men, lack of understanding by the good, the hatred of the wicked, and sometimes persecution by both the good and the wicked.

And yet how much suffering is wasted that could help to redeem souls! How many potential hosts will never be offered up or united to the great and only Host! There is an efficacious apostolate, and great charity as well, in showing to those who suffer—perhaps to no purpose— in hospital wards or sickrooms, the divine value of their suffering when endured in communion with the sufferings of the Lamb of God!

And high up on this steep path of suffering, there are the great trials by which God Himself takes over the task of purifying the soul, plunging it into a sea of bitterness and sorrow. This is the privilege of souls destined for great holiness and powerful apostolic action. Like a probing fire, the justice and holiness of God penetrate the soul with a jealous flame that melts away all the rust of its human impurities. To quote Father Bernadot: "Desolations mark the soul with the stamp of perfection and imprint upon it the closest likeness to Christ. They proceed directly from God. Their source is His infinite sanctity; their immediate cause the mysterious and awful workings of the Holy Spirit, who desires to make the soul participate in the eternal and sovereign Purity: for this end it is seized, despoiled, broken, abandoned, seized again, plunged into bitterness, tested by a thousand trials until the transformation is complete. . . . At such times everything is painful, even the thoughts of graces formerly received, for the Holy Spirit diffuses in the soul a secret and most pure light which manifesting on the one hand the greatness of God, on the other its own misery and nothingness, casts everything else into an intense gloom, destroys all natural consolations, establishes a desolate solitude in the presence of the Most Holy, and plunges the soul in a terrible spiritual darkness, even into a condition of terror and anguish. It is thus that God purifies the soul completely, for 'our God is a consuming fire' (Heb. 12:29)." [35]

In spite of appearances to the contrary, this is the closest possible union with Jesus in His immolation, a communion with the anguish that seized Him at Gethsemani when He cried out as if He were wavering: "My soul is sad, even unto death!" [36] It is a communion with Christ's mysterious dereliction on the Cross which made Him cry out to His Father: "My God, My God, why hast Thou forsaken Me?" [37] The only attitude to be taken by the soul thus put to the test is that of uniting its abandonment, through heroic faith, to that of the divine Master and of standing firm under God's temptations,[38] without

[35] M.-V. Bernadot, O.P., *From Holy Communion to the Blessed Trinity*, pp. 81–82.
[36] Matt. 26:38.          [37] *Ibid.*, 27:46.          [38] Cf. Ecclus. 2:3.

ever doubting His love. "In these trials the soul has simply to hold herself firmly united to Jesus, and by the wounds of His sacred humanity she will penetrate to the divinity." [39]

Once the painful trial is over, the soul will find itself transformed into God, filled with good things, and capable of communicating to others the graces with which it has been favored. Like Christ, the servant of Yahveh, this soul "shall see a long-lived seed and the will of the Lord shall be prosperous in his hand." [40] This is the ultimate explanation of certain lives tormented by unspeakable sufferings, filled with untold trials, with true interior martyrdoms whose visible and exterior crosses were but the shadow. Those whom the Lord judges capable of passing through this crucible belong to the race of the saints, of those who exercise a powerful and enduring action within the bosom of the Church and lead a legion of predestined souls to God. To them can be applied what St. Paul said of Christ: "For it became Him for whom all things and through whom are all things, . . . to perfect through sufferings the author of their salvation." [41]

The founders of religious orders, the great reformers, the outstanding Pontiffs of the Church, all the saints, especially those whose apostolic and supernatural influence has been deepest and most extensive—all have been among the privileged sufferers, those friends of the Crucified who have carried their cross in His footsteps and consummated their immolation with Him on a new Calvary. St. Francis of Assisi, St. John of the Cross, St. Teresa of Avila, St. John Vianney, and many others drank the chalice of the Passion in union with Jesus. In them have been verified God's words with regard to Christ:

[39] M.-V. Bernadot, O.P., *op. cit.*, pp. 84–85.    [40] Isa. 53:10.
[41] Heb. 2:10.

"Because His soul hath labored, He shall see and be filled:
by His knowledge shall this My just servant justify many,
and He shall bear their iniquities." [42]

Such is the completion of our life-giving union with our
divine Redeemer. Begun through baptism by the first grace
of incorporation into Christ Jesus, strengthened by the
action of the other sacraments, vocal prayer, the liturgy,
and mental prayer, it gradually extends to our whole life
and then aspires to be communicated to others so that all
redeemed men may give themselves to Him who won them
at the price of His blood and may receive from Him the
divine life that He possesses in its fullness, the life of faith
and love, and thus glorify the Father in union with Him.

"We feel immense desires for apostolic action; we want
to make Him known and loved so that He may be praised;
we want to sanctify souls more and more so that their
praise may become more and more agreeable to God. And
we exercise this apostolate by dwelling very simply in
Him. In that divine fire, we hold all the souls of the entire
world. What we do, we do in the name of all. I like to say
the *Our Father,* united at once to Jesus and the world. By
uniting myself to the souls of all men it seems to me that I
am offering up universal praise; by uniting myself to Jesus
I make this praise infinite in each one." [43]

Is this not the fulfillment of Jesus' prayer: "that they
. . . may be one in us, . . . that they may be perfected in
unity"? [44] Perfect consummation in the unity of the Mystical Body through life-giving union with Christ the Savior, with a view to bringing back the whole world to God,
so that at last He "may be all in all" [45]—such is the innermost hope of every soul that lives fully in Christ Jesus.

[42] Isa. 53:11.                    [43] *Consummata* by Father Raoul Plus, S.J.
[44] John 17:21, 23.                [45] I Cor. 15:28.

## TEXTS FOR MEDITATION

[Father,] I have manifested Thy name to the men whom Thou hast given Me out of the world. They were Thine, and Thou hast given them to Me, and they have kept Thy word. Now they have learnt that whatever Thou hast given Me is from Thee; because the words that Thou hast given Me I have given to them. And they have received them, and have known of a truth that I came forth from Thee, and they have believed that Thou didst send Me.

I pray for them; . . . I am no longer in the world, but these are in the world, and I am coming to Thee. Holy Father, keep in Thy name those whom Thou hast given Me, that they may be one even as We are. While I was with them, I kept them in Thy name. Those whom Thou hast given Me I guarded; and not one of them perished except the son of perdition, in order that the Scripture might be fulfilled.

But now I am coming to Thee; and these things I speak in the world, in order that they may have My joy made full in themselves. I have given them Thy word; and the world has hated them, because they are not of the world, even as I am not of the world.

I do not pray that Thou take them out of the world, but that Thou keep them from evil. They are not of the world, even as I am not of the world. Sanctify them in the truth. Thy word is truth.

Even as Thou hast sent Me into the world, so I also have sent them into the world. And for them I sanctify Myself, that they also may be sanctified in truth. (John 17:6–19.)

Souls that are aflame cannot remain inactive. No doubt, like St. Magdalen, they stay at Jesus' feet, listening to His gentle and flaming words. While they appear to give nothing, they give much more than Martha, who frets about many things.

On the other hand, it was not Martha's labors that Jesus blamed, but only her anxiety. . . .

All the saints have understood this, and perhaps those who have filled the universe with the light of the doctrine of the Gospel understood it better than the rest. Was it not during prayer that St. Paul, St. Augustine, St. Thomas Aquinas, St. John of the Cross, St. Teresa, and so many other friends of God have drawn this admirable science that delights the greatest geniuses?

A scientist has said: Give me a lever, a fulcrum, and I shall lift the world. What Archimedes was unable to obtain because his request had only a material goal and was not addressed to God, the saints have received in full. The Almighty has given them a fulcrum: Himself, Himself alone! As a lever, mental prayer which kindles a fire of love; and that is how they lifted the world, that is how the saints who are still militant lift it and will continue to lift it until the end of time. (St. Thérèse of Lisieux.)

Receive, O my God, the renewed gift that I offer You of myself, of my soul and my life, wishing to love and serve You alone, joyously, everywhere, always, with my whole being; wishing to do Your will completely, in sickness or in health, in poverty or in riches, in happiness or in suffering, in life or in death, and asking you simply to make use of me as the lowliest of instruments for the good of souls and for Your glory.

Through me, may pain, supernatural joy, my whole life and even my death loudly affirm the grandeur of divine love, the holiness of the Church, the tenderness and gentleness of the Heart of Jesus, the existence and beauty of the supernatural life, the reality of our Christian hope.

I believe, I adore, I place myself under the special protection of the Blessed Virgin, and I have the sweet trust that, offered up by her, my humble oblation will, through divine grace, serve the Church, souls, and those who are so very dear to me here below. (Elizabeth Leseur.)

CHAPTER 14 ✒

# Fruits of Life

A DOCTRINE of life such as we have presented must not remain in the domain of speculation. It must be put into practice. After it has penetrated the soul, it must be translated into "works of God." [1]

Every aspect of supernatural truth tends in one way or another to enrich the life of the soul and make it fruitful. Jesus said: "The words that I have spoken to you are spirit and life." [2] It is, therefore, to the supreme interest of souls aspiring to greater holiness that the treasures of Scripture and theology be placed within their reach. More than any other, the doctrine of our union with the humanity of Christ is of a nature to bring forth in us the abundance of life that our Lord came to give us. [3]

We should meditate upon this doctrine with a lively and practical faith in order to form a truly Christian mentality, a way of thinking and judging, of willing and acting, which is in harmony with the central mystery of the Incarnation of the Word and its unlimited sanctifying power. In pointing out practical conclusions to this doctrine, we shall present certain basic maxims for a spirituality of union with God through a more explicit and conscious recourse to the life-giving humanity of Christ.

[1] John 6:28.     [2] *Ibid.*, 6:64.     [3] Cf. *Ibid.*, 10:10.

We have said more conscious and more explicit. Every Christian spirituality—to be more exact, each of the various forms of the one and only Christian spirituality—is founded on Jesus Christ, the Word Incarnate, who is the only source of salvation, as St. Peter says in the Acts of the Apostles: "Neither is there salvation in any other." [4] And in the words of St. Paul: "For other foundation no one can lay, but that which has been laid [by God Himself], which is Christ Jesus." [5] But we can delve into this treasure in many different ways and never exhaust its riches. From age to age Christian souls will continue to discover in it new spiritual resources; "things new and old," [6] as our Lord has said. The dogma of the humanity of the Word, as an instrument of grace and source of life in its every act and mystery, contains infinite possibilities and virtualities for the renewal and sanctification of souls. For Christ Jesus "has become for us God-given wisdom, and justice, and sanctification and redemption." [7]

Let us draw up some practical conclusions or resolutions that will help us make the best possible use of these pages and live by the truths they set forth.

First, a preliminary and general resolution: We must learn to know the riches of life which Christ holds for us; we must study them by reading, meditation, and the exercise of our faith.

St. Paul was always reverting to this matter. We know with what zeal he strove to communicate to his faithful the science of Christ, the Christian wisdom which is the principle of all holiness. Writing to the Ephesians, he said: "I . . . do not cease to give thanks for you, making mention of you in my prayers, that the God of our Lord Jesus

---

[4] Acts 4:12.          [5] I Cor. 3:11.          [6] Matt. 13:52.
[7] I Cor. 1:30.

Christ, the Father of glory, may grant you the spirit of wisdom and revelation in deep knowledge of Him: the eyes of your mind being enlightened, so that you may know what is the hope of His calling, what the riches of the glory of His inheritance in the saints." [8]

We must remember that the life of grace enters our souls through the door of faith, through our supernatural understanding of the mystery of God and Christ. Therefore, anyone who is eager to live his Christian life to the full, in an ever closer and more fruitful union with Jesus, will delight in reading and re-reading the works that tell us of this life through Christ and of its countless manifestations.[9] And going beyond human authors, he will quench his thirst at the wellsprings of Holy Scripture and above all of the Gospel, which shows us Jesus living among us, saving us, and sanctifying us even by His slightest actions. He will turn to the Epistles of St. Paul, St. Peter, and St. John, which all teach us how to actualize the Gospel of Christ within the framework of our life.

If we are going to let Jesus live within us, we must be willing to die to ourselves, and to accomplish this work of renunciation in union with Jesus who died for us on the Cross. Without death to self, no interior life can attain its full stature. Spiritual growth soon stops and brings forth only a puny flower that will soon be choked by weeds, brambles, and thorns; by the tangled network of our passions, sentiments, and unruly moods. Jesus calls us to follow

[8] Eph. 1:15–18.

[9] We would suggest the following works: Dom Marmion's *Christ the Life of the Soul;* Raoul Plus, S.J., *In Christ Jesus,* and *Christ in His Brethren;* Marie-Vincent Bernadot, O.P., *Our Lady in Our Life,* and *From Holy Communion to the Blessed Trinity;* Paul de Jaegher, *One With Jesus;* Sister Elizabeth of the Trinity, *Reminiscences;* and Emil Mersch, S.J., *Morality and the Mystical Body.*

Him, but the first condition He posits is abnegation: "If anyone wishes to come after Me, let him deny himself." [10]

But abnegation must be conceived in a Christian climate, in an atmosphere of union through love. For love is the strongest force to draw the soul along the paths of generosity and renunciation. By its innate power, true love frees the soul from many attachments that are incompatible with love. We would do well in this connection to call to mind the method which St. Thérèse used so successfully, a method that was at once deeply theological and psychologically sound.[11]

Abnegation calls for the virtue of humility as its necessary complement. The soul that wants to live by Christ's life will quite naturally be humble. It will tend to efface itself to make room for the divine Master and to repeat with the holy Precursor: "He must increase, but I must decrease." [12]

The great obstacle to the life of Jesus in us is the expansion of the ego, which so easily happens even in souls that claim to be Christian. The soul that has a sincere desire to let Christ live within itself, strives with all its might to disappear and to kill its egotism. In the words of Father de Jaegher: "Does not such a soul, each day of her life, ardently desire to be nothing, but that Jesus should be all in her? From the day when she resolved to substitute Jesus for self, to identify herself with Christ, she has known no other ambition or ideal. She surrendered herself once and for all to humility." [13]

The Mass must regain its full significance for the soul

---

[10] Matt. 16:24.

[11] Cf. *The Spirit of St. Thérèse* (London: Burns Oates, 1948.)

[12] John 3:30.

[13] Paul de Jaegher, S.J., *One with Jesus* (Westminster, Md.: The Newman Press, 1955), pp. 22–23.

as the sacrifice of Jesus united to His Church. The Christian must offer himself with all the faith and generous love of his soul, together with Jesus, in homage to God and place his whole life upon the altar with the sacred Host. This offering will become specific and detailed according to the needs of the moment: in the acceptance of a given sacrifice, in the immolation of an attachment, in the will to correct a certain fault, to make a particular effort, to do a work of charity, or to engage in a given apostolic action. But none of these things will ever make us lose sight of the principal oblation, namely, Christ, immolated on the Cross for the glory of the Father, for our sins and weaknesses, for our needs and indigence, and drawing us toward Himself to make of our whole being "a sacrifice, living, holy, pleasing to God." [14]

Eucharistic Communion will be, as much as possible, the natural corollary of our participation in the divine Sacrifice. Desire for Holy Communion is continually reborn in the soul that is eager for union with God and with our Lord. The host of the sacrifice has become for us "the Bread of life." Regardless of the other means for living with Jesus, and regardless of our efforts to maintain a lifegiving contact with the divine Master in the midst of our occupations, we must begin with the Eucharistic union. By frequent Communion we yield ourselves to the mysterious and transforming action of the heavenly food. We must, so to speak, tap the high-voltage current that the Sacrament of the altar places at our disposal. Without this Sacrament, as Jesus has told us, we cannot have life within us.[15] Granted this fact, we shall regulate the frequency of our Communions in accordance with the time at our disposal, our nearness to a church or chapel, and the duties

[14] Rom. 12:1.          [15] Cf. John 6:54.

of our state of life. And if frequent Communion requires us to make a real effort to get up earlier and to readjust the schedule of our day, our hunger for the Host will give us the courage to do it.

There is no profound life without mental prayer. Christ cannot grow in us if we do not maintain contact with Him in the intimacy and recollection of prolonged, silent prayer which gives the divine Master the leisure to penetrate our soul and its faculties with His grace and to reveal Himself to us in the light of contemplation. This rule of the spiritual life receives so much support from the teaching of the masters, the experience of souls, and the example of the saints, that we need not insist further upon it.

Various adaptations may well be necessary with respect to the duration of mental prayer, or the place and the manner in which it is carried on, depending upon the circumstances of each one's life. There can be no doubt, however, of the need for mental prayer in one form or another in every deeply Christian life. Ordinarily, our life will be only as good as our mental prayer. The other means of union with Jesus—the Mass, Communion, the liturgical life—bear their fruit in proportion to the recollection of the soul and its life of mental prayer.

The great master of the life of union with Christ, Dom Marmion, is very explicit on this point: "The means we have of ever tending to God and remaining united to Him —the sacraments, Mass, the Divine Office, the life of obedience and labor—only attain the summum of their efficacy if we lead a life of prayer. . . . A soul that does not live this habitual life of prayer needs a great effort each time it wants to be recollected and to arouse the affections upon which, generally speaking, depends the fruitfulness of the supernatural means we have for sanctifying ourselves." [16]

We must then go from the altar to our home, from the sanctuary to our places of work, without any moral break, without loss of contact, and reach the point where we never act alone but set about all our tasks in union with Him, "hand in hand" with Jesus. Father de Jaegher develops this essential point as follows: "To go with Him to prayer, to good works, to my daily duties, to association with my neighbor, to the most indifferent actions, such as my meals." [17] It is in our daily activities that overwork, the great enemy of our life of union with Jesus, is always ready to assault us. This is truer today than at any other time. There is so much to do that we have to be quick and not lose any time. We cannot remain "lost" in devotion. Certainly not. But we can always remain in Christ: "Abide in Me." [18] Unless we do this our works will be sterile for eternal life, both for the eternal life of the souls we are cultivating and for our own eternal life. Our Lord has told us: "Without Me you can do nothing." [19] Those who do not abide in Him will be like branches broken off from the vine and will bear no fruit of life.

This is the secret of all who have ever accomplished works that were fruitful for the Church and for the world. But it calls for a firm will and continual watchfulness lest we become totally engrossed in exterior matters and exhaust all the vitality of our interior life. Periodic halts, monthly recollections, terms of study, and retreats are intended to bring us face to face with our great ideal and to

---

[16] *Christ the Ideal of the Monk,* translated by a nun of Tyburn Convent (St. Louis: B. Herder, 1926), p. 341.

[17] *One with Jesus,* p. 45.     [18] John 15:4.

[19] *Ibid.,* 15:5.

immerse us once again in the vital center of our life: Christ Himself, contemplated, loved, and served in all things.

Devotion to the duties of our state of life will foster our spirituality of union with Christ by making us look upon even our dullest activities, not as chores imposed upon us from without, but as manifestations of the will of God. We shall always bear in mind the fact that Jesus vowed His life to God's will and that even today He continues to accomplish His Father's will through us, His mystical members.

Jesus' rule of life was the will of His Father. He loved to say: "This is why I have been sent." [20] And again: "For this is the will of My Father who sent Me." [21] Our "mission" can be nothing else but a continuation of Jesus' mission. Our course of action lies in carrying out the efficacious will of God who, through Christ, influences and commands all our actions with a view to making us cooperate in the fulfillment of His designs of love. St. Paul reminds us of this in many ways: "He predestined us to be adopted through Jesus Christ as His sons, according to the purpose of His will." [22] Again: "That He may make known to us the mystery of His will according to His good pleasure [which is] . . . to re-establish all things in Christ, both those in the heavens and those on the earth." [23] The Apostle shows us the manifestation of the designs of Providence, which "works all things according to the counsel of His will, to contribute to the praise of His glory." [24]

We accomplish the great plans of God for us by bowing, in union with the beloved Son, to all the wishes of the Father in all our actions, from the most trifling to those that fulfill our most serious duties. We fulfill God's plans

[20] Luke 4:43.　　　[21] John 6:40.　　　[22] Eph. 1:5.
[23] Eph. 1:9-10.　　　[24] *Ibid.*, 1:11-12.

by communing constantly with the loving submission of Jesus and by saying with Him: "Father, Thy will be done!"

It is through *love* that we shall strive to accomplish the all-wise and beneficent will of God. Love must be the soul of our life. Jesus declared on the eve of His death: "The world [must] know that I love the Father." [25] And His great commandment, drawn from the Old Testament, is this: "Thou shalt love the Lord thy God with thy whole heart and with thy whole soul, and with thy whole mind." [26] St. Thérèse of Lisieux commented on this with the words: "My director, who is Jesus, does not teach me to count my acts; He teaches me to do all things through love." [27] Is not love the best incentive to this life of union with Jesus and, conversely, must not union with Him through self-forgetfulness develop into an uninterrupted love of the Father who is in heaven? The soul that is united to Christ will love through the heart of Jesus.

To use the words of Father de Jaegher: "At each hour of the day she offers to the Father the actions, the prayers, the sufferings, the loving aspirations, the desires which Jesus produces in her, and which are like so many expressions of her love for God. . . . She offers herself unceasingly in union with the heart of Jesus, who is Himself the infinite source of her love." [28]

The soul united to Jesus repeats with St. Paul: "The love of Christ impels us." [29]

We must desire ever more ardently to reveal to others Christ's love for us and to communicate to them our love for Him. United to Jesus, we must be His apostles and

[25] John 14:31.  [26] Matt. 22:37; cf. also Deut. 6:5.
[27] *Lettres de sainte Thérèse de l'Enfant-Jesus* (Lisieux, 1948), p. 223.
[28] *Op. cit.*, p. 19.  [29] II Cor. 5:14.

draw the whole world to God as much as we can by the
conquering power of our fraternal charity, by a Christian
life that is a witness and a light for those who are still in
darkness, by persuasive words, compelling example, and by
the suffering that fructifies the hidden work of Christ's
grace within souls.

When we give the riches of grace to others, we possess
these riches twice over. We increase our own treasure and
attain to a better understanding of the demands of the
divine life, which pours itself out through the practice of
the apostolic virtues such as kindness, self-forgetfulness,
and generous immolation. Let us, therefore, imitate the
Good Shepherd, who gave His life for His sheep [30] and
who taught us that the greatest proof of our love is to lay
down our life for our friends.[31]

The apostolic orientation of our life is an answer to the
Church's pressing invitation and to the obvious need of
souls and a world on the brink of disaster. But we must
carry on our apostolate through prayer, under the eye of
Jesus and under the impulse of His love. Moreover, each
of us must perform his apostolic work within the framework of his own individual circumstances, in harmony with
the duties of his state of life, and in the environment where
Providence has placed him for its own special reasons.

Mary, the Mother of divine grace, formed Jesus in her
womb and continues to form Him in each of us. She can
best initiate us to the life of union with Christ, for she will
always be the perfect model of this life. Under her tutelage,
our whole Christian life will develop in a Marian climate.
Hence, we must never look upon our devotion to Mary as
a secondary practice, juxtaposed to our life in Jesus, en-
croaching upon it and impeding its growth. On the con-

[30] Cf. John 10:11.          [31] Cf. *Ibid.,* 15:13.

trary, enlightened faith will see in devotion to Mary another expression of our life with Christ. The resources of Mary, who is indissolubly united to her Son, will enrich and broaden our own life, for Mary lived in all perfection the life "hidden with Christ in God" [32] which St. Paul has set up as the Christian ideal.

Of course, our Marian life can have many diverse expressions. Each of us may freely follow in this matter the inspirations of the Spirit of Jesus, for He is also the Spirit of Mary. Let us take advantage of the suggestions of the liturgy, which celebrates so many feasts of the Blessed Virgin Mary, from the Annunciation—the supreme mystery of the vital union between Christ and His Mother—to the Assumption, and most recently, the Queenship of Mary. In the cycle of these Marian feasts, the life-giving influence of the divine Mediatrix is more perfectly revealed to us in its close bond to the mysteries of the one Mediator. The writings of the saints will help give form and substance to our devotion to Mary. Chief among these writings should be mentioned St. Alphonsus Liguori's *The Glories of Mary* and St. Louis-Marie de Montfort's *Treatise on the True Devotion to the Blessed Virgin.*[33]

To enter fully into this Marian life, we shall want to understand and delight in the Rosary, relive its sanctifying mysteries in union with Jesus and Mary, and meditate on the admirable prayers of the *Our Father,* the *Hail Mary,* the *Gloria,* and the *Credo,* which make up its mystical crown. To the Rosary as well as to many other secrets of

[32] Col. 3:3.

[33] Without wishing to detract from other splendid works on the Blessed Virgin, we should like to call the attention of our readers to a little jewel of Marian piety that fits in with the doctrinal emphasis of the present book, namely, Father Emil Neubert's *My Ideal, Jesus, Son of Mary* (Milwaukee: Bruce, 1936).

the spiritual life, the following words of Jesus apply: "I praise Thee, Father, Lord of heaven and earth, that Thou didst hide these things from the wise and prudent, and didst reveal them to little ones." [34] Blessed spiritual littleness, that enables us to penetrate the mysterious depths of the Holy Rosary and thus commune with the joys, sorrows, and glories of Christ and of His Virgin Mother!

In the Rosary we shall find once again all our Christian faith and all dogmatic and moral theology. We shall even find the loftiest paths of union with God, for these paths are nothing else but the way that Christ and the Blessed Virgin have blazed for us in the work of our Redemption. It is by following the road that goes from the Incarnation of the Word to the Ascension of Christ and to the glorious Assumption and Coronation of His Mother, passing through the painful ascent of Calvary, that we shall gradually be united to the sacred humanity of the Savior, become conformed to His image [35] according to the Father's will, and thus realize our eternal predestination. The Rosary, which Mary came from heaven several times to give to us, will become the "bands of love" [36] of which the prophet speaks, and which Mary mercifully holds out to her children to draw and attach them to Christ and to God.

[34] Matt. 11:25.                    [35] Cf. Rom. 8:29.
[36] Osee 11:4: "I will draw them with the cords of Adam, and with the bands of love."